MW01116236

A Collection Of Wisdom Quotes, Proverbs, Wise Thoughts

A Collection Of Wisdom Quotes, Proverbs, Wise Thoughts
Demetrios Konstantinos Prapas

—

Published by - Spines
ISBN: 979-8-89383-531-1

A Collection Of Wisdom Quotes, Proverbs, Wise Thoughts

Demetrios Konstantinos Prapas

ACKNOWLEDGMENTS

I would like to express my appreciation to all my international friends and colleagues for their feedback, encouraging to write and publish this book.

PREFACE

I believe this book will offer you a special knowledge to deal with daily challenges, make wise decisions, think life is too short to worry so much, think positive, smell the coffee and enjoy your life. This is a result of an old hobby to collect quotes, wisdom thoughts phrases, wise example from newspapers, media, and books. I made an extra effort to search for their originality (some countries, ethnic & religious groups, CEOs, presidents, celebrities, and media (i.e., Facebook and Tik Tok), etc. claimed for them owns) and tried to give credits to the sources and to the original authors. However, there are some quotes or sayings with unknown authors (anonymous).

The purpose of life is not to be happy. It is to be useful, to be honorable, to have it make some difference that you have lived well. - Ralph Waldo Emerson

There are three things you can do with your life: You can waste it, you can spend it, or you can invest it. The best use of your life is to invest it in something that will last longer than your time on Earth. - Rick Warren

A single day among the learned lasts longer than the longer life of the ignorant. – Posidonius

Life is too short to waste your time on people who don't respect, appreciate, and value you. Spend your life with people who make you smile, laugh, and feel loved. - Roger Lee

Life is a circle of happiness, sadness, hard times, and good times. If you are going through hard times, faith that good times are not the way. - Buddha

The only wealth you will keep forever is the wealth you have given away. – Marcus Aurelius

Life is so precious. Every day is a gift so Make it Count! You have purpose and this world needs you. I don't know what you are going through, but today is a fresh start! - Vick Tipries

. . .

Sometimes in life, your situation will keep repeating itself until you learn your lesson. – Brigitte Nicole

One of the best lessons you can learn in life is to master how to remain calm. – Catherine Pulsifer

No one stays with you permanently, so learn to survive alone. - Denis Agaba

To create the life of your dreams, the time has come to love you. Focus on your joy. Do all the things that make you feel good. Love you inside and out. Everything will change in your life, when you chance the inside of you. Allow the Universe to give you every good thing you deserve by being a magnet to them all. To be a magnet for every single thing you deserve you must be a Brooks Davis magnet pf love. - Rhonda Byrne

Remember: you are dying every day. – Seneca

I refuse to go through life explaining myself and defending my decisions to everyone. This is my life. I am going to live it my way. No apologies, no regrets. - Rabina Mughal

Self-control is strength. Calmness is mastery. You have to get to a point where your mood doesn't shift based on the insignificant actions of someone else. Don't allow others to control the direction of your life. Don't allow your emotions to overpower your intelligence. – Morgan Freeman

. . .

To bear trials with a calm mind robs misfortune of its strength and burden. - Seneca

An angry man opens his mouth and shuts his eyes. – Cato

Don't tell people what you're going to do. Do it and shock them. And after shocking them, stay silent. Move onto your next project. - Leonardo DiCaprio

The most dangerous people to you are not strangers, but your friends, family and partners. They know your weaknesses, failures and secrets and can use them against you. They know where, how, and when to attack you that will cause the greatest damage. Watch your back. Keep your plans private. Move in silence. - Rybina Mughal

Life is going to test you every day not to punish you but to train you to have strength for another day and guide you to become the warrior that you were meant to be. – Roger Lee

Loyalty is hard to find, trust is easy to lose, and actions speak louder than words. Look out for the people who look out for you. Loyalty is everything. – Morgan Freeman

Don't let anyone break you. There may always be people who secretly want to see you fail. That's okay. Just stay strong and stand tall. - Kristen Butter

. . .

Calm brings inner strength and self-confidence, so that's very important for good health. - Dalai Lama

Nothing last forever. That means the hardships ad the pain you are going through right now won't stay forever either. That means you'll find a way to heal. Remember, life has its reasons, one after another they arrive and they leave. You may feel like you won't' survive this season of pain, the strangles you are dealing with, but I assure you, you will. Like these seasons of life your circumstances will change too. And I hope that this period of change makes you realize your inner power, the incredible strength of your heart too. – Dhiman

You're not defined by your past; you're prepared by it. You're stronger, more experienced, and you have greater confidence. - Joel Osteen

You will never reach your destination, if you stop and throw stones at every dog that barks. - Winston Churchill

Standing up for yourself doesn't make you argumentive. Sharing your feelings doesn't make you oversensitive. And saying no doesn't make you uncaring or selfish. If someone won't respect your feelings, needs and boundaries, the problem isn't you; it's them. - Lori Deschene

I'm not upset that you lied to me, I'm upset that from now on I can't believe you. – Nietzsche

. . .

A bird does not sing because it has an answer. He sings because it has a song. - Joan Aknglund

Discipline is listening to people tell you what to do, where to be, to do something. Sel-discipline is knowing that you are responsible for everything that happens in your life; you are the only one who can take yourself to the desired heights. – Adam Schefter-Mike Shangham

Don't let the behavior of others destroy your inner peace. - Dalai Lama

The mind is everything. What you think, you become. - Buddha

The mind is everything. What you think, you become. – Buddha

We become not a melting pot, but a beautiful mosaic. Different people, different beliefs, different yearnings, different hopes, different dreams. - Jimmy Carter

Nothing is more honorable than a grateful heart. - Seneca

Bring whenever you go. Shine light whenever it's dark. Leave blessing whenever you've been. Be kind whenever you are. - Mary Davis

. . .

When you feel powerless, that's because you stopped listening to your heart, that's where the power comes from. - Gianni Crow

Enjoy yourself, it's later than you think. – Socrates

Don' suffer imagined troubles. – Seneca

We are not our best intentions. We are what we do. - Amy Dickinson

Do me this favor. I won't forget it. Ask your friends in the neighborhood about me. They'll tell you I know how to return a favor. - Vito Corleone

If you in your comfort zone, that's where you'll fail. Success is not a comfortable procedure. It is a very uncomfortable thing to attempt. So, you got to get comfortable being uncomfortable, if you ever wanna be successful, start putting some pressure on, put some pressure on yourself. - Steve Harvey

Comfort is the worst addiction. – Marcus Aurelius

Don't be afraid to start again. This time, you're not starting from scratch, you're starting from experience. - Peter Hayden Dinklage

The world will ask who you are, and if you do not know, the world will tell you. - Carl Jung

. . .

When people walk away from you, let them go. Your destiny is never tied to anyone who leaves you, and it doesn't mean they are bad people. It just means their part in your story is over. - T.D. Jakes

Treat success and failure the same. – Marcus Aurelius

Love your fate. – Epictetus

The greatest way to live with honor in this world is to what we pretend to be. – Socrates

I hope you find the courage to start again. I hope even if you struggle to find your way sometimes, you will hold onto life, you will not give up on your life. I hope you will choose hope and all the things that make you believe that the possibilities in this life are endless, that when a door takes you to a dead end, you will somehow find a new one, you will discover your true strength. – Bhima

I begin to speak only when I'm certain what I'll say isn't better left unsaid. – Cato

In a little while, you, will have forgotten everything in a little while, everything will have forgotten you. – Marcus Aurelius

. . .

Uncertainty is an uncomfortable position. But certainty is an absurd one. – Voltaire

When you're good at something, you'll tell everyone. When you're great at something, they'll tell you. – Walter Payton

It does not matter how slowly you go as long as you do not stop. - Confucius

Be a free thinker and don't accept everything you her as truth. Be critical and evaluate what you believe in. - Aristotle.

The way to get started is to quit talking and begin doing. – Walt Disney

Victory is reserved for those who are willing to pay the price. – Sun Tzu

It may seem difficult at first but everything is difficult at first. – Musashi

People who say it cannot be done should not interrupt those who are doing it. - Bernard Shaw.

Someone is sitting in the shade today because someone planted a tree a long time ago. - Warren Buffet

. . .

One loyal friend is better than ten thousand relatives. - Euripides

Pause before judging. Pause before accusing. Pause before assuming. Pause whenever you're about to react harshly, and you'll avoid doing and saying things you will regret later. - Lori Deschene

We are like many pellets of intense falling on the same alter. Some collapse sooner, others later, but it makes no difference. – Marcus Aurelius

I've learned that no matter what happens, or how bad it seems today, life does go on and it will belter tomorrow. – Maya Angelou

Learn to be silent. Let your quiet mind listen and absorb. - Pythagoras

The problem with the world is that intelligent people are full of doubts and stupid ones are full if confidence. - Charles Bukewski

The only beautiful path is the one you create. – Maxine Lagace

It's never too late to reinvent yourself. – Marc Russell Scarioni

The biggest lesson that I've learn is that things can change so quickly, never get used to one thing because everything can flip on its head. – Santan Dave

. . .

The greatest prison people live in is the fear of what other people think. – David Icke

Knowing yourself is the beginning of wisdom. - Aristotle

Open your mind before your mouth. - Aristophanes

Appear weak when you are strong. And strong, when you are weak. - Sun Tzu

Time you enjoy wasting, was not wasted. - Bertrand Russell

Don't allow your past or present condition to control you. It's just a process that you're going through to get you to the next level. - T.D. Jakes

Live as if you were to die tomorrow. Learn as if you were to live forever. - Mahatma Gandhi

There are only two ways to live your life. One is as though nothing is a miracle. The other is as though everything is a miracle. - Albert Einstein

Two things to remember in life: "Take care your thoughts when you are alone" and "take care of your words when you are with people." - Monique

. . .

Don't let anyone break you. There may always be people who secretly want you see you fail. That's okay. Just stay strong and stay tall. – Kristen Butler

I forgive, but I also learn a lesson I won't hate you, but I'll never get close enough for you to hurt me again. I can't let my forgiveness become foolishness. - Tony Gaskins

Only focus on what's in control. – Epictetus

Just do one thing every day. – Zeno

And she embraced chaos as she painted her life with purpose. - J H Hard

I have learned that people will forget what you've said. People forget what you did. But people will never forget how you them feel. - Maya Angelou

The meaning of life is to find your gift. The purpose of life is to give it away. - Pablo Picasso

When I despair, I remember that all through history the way of truth and love have always won. There have been tyrants and murderers, and for a time, they can seem invincible, but in the end, they always fall. Think of it, always. - Mahatma Gandhi

. . .

Above all, don't lie to yourself. The man who lies to himself and listens to his own lie comes to a point that he cannot distinguish the truth within him, or around him, and so loses all respect for himself and for others. And having no respect he ceases to love. - Fyodor Dostoevsky

A fool is known by his speech, and a wise man by silence. – Pythagoras

One of the most important things I've learned in life is to ignore most of what people say. I watch what they do instead. – Amanda Patterson

I am still learning how to go back and reread my own chapters without feeling like I want to set all of my pages on fire. – E.V. Rogina

Life is a succession of lessons which must be lived to be understood. – Helen Keller

You're never wrong, if you love and help people. – Maxine Legace

The biggest lesson I learned this year is not force anything; conversations, friendships, relationships, attention, love. Anything forced is just not worth fighting for, whatever flows, flows. What crashes, crashes. – Amanda Rose

. . .

Care about what other people think and you will always be their prisoner. – Lao Tzu

The one thing that I keep learning over and over again is that I don't know nothing. I mean, that that's my life lesson. – Dwayne Jonhson

Be the change that you wish to see in the world. - Mahatma Gandhi

Honesty, I don't have time to hate people who hate me, because I'm too busy loving people who love me. - Denis Agaba

Honesty is a very expensive gift. Don't expect it from cheap people. - Denis Agaba

The truth is, unless you let go, unless you forgive yourself, unless you forgive the situation, unless you realize that the situation is over, you cannot move forward. - Steve Maraboli,

Never be afraid to raise your voice for honesty and truth and compassion against injustice and lying and greed. If people all over the world would do this, it would change the earth. - William Faulkner

Leaders are innovative, entrepreneurial, and future-oriented. They focus on getting the job done. - Brian Tracy

. . .

Never tell your problems to everyone. 80% don't care and the other 20% are glad you have them. – Pable Escobar

The experience of pain or loss can be formidably motivating force. – John C. Maxwell

Darkness cannot drive out darkness: only light can do that. Hate cannot drive out hate: only love can do that. - Martin Luther King Jr.

Never forget what you are. The rest of the world will not. Wear it like armor, and it can never be used to hurt you. - Tyrion Lannister

A man with no motive is a man no one suspects. Always keep your foes confused. If they are never certain who you are or what you want, they cannon know what you are likely to do next. - Pentyl Baelish

Pay attention to your enemies, for they are the first to discover your mistakes. - Antisthenes

Education is the greatest manifestation of the innate potential of the human mind. – Abhijit Naskar

Only the dead have seen the end of war. – Plato

. . .

Our greatest glory is not in never falling, but in rising every time we fall. – Confucius

Do not dwell in the past, do not dream of the future, concentrate the mind on the present moment. -Buddha

The mind is not a vessel to be filled, but a fir to be kindled. – Plutarch

It is the power of the mind to be unconquerable. - Seneca

The energy of the mind is the essence of life. - Aristotle

Always remember, your focus determines your reality. – George Lucas

The successful warrior is the average man with a laser-like focus. – Bruce Lee

Successful people maintain a positive focus in life no matter what is going on around them. - Jack Carfield

The image you create in your mind, is a choice your life will follow. - Kabelo Mabona

. . .

To create the life of your dreams, the time has come to love you. Focus on your joy. Do all the things that make you feel good. Love you inside and out. Everything will change in your life, when you chance the inside of you. Allow the Universe to give you every good thing you deserve by being a magnet to them all. To be a magnet for every single thing you deserve you must be a Brooks Davis magnet of love. - Rhonda Byrne

Dreams don't have to just be dreams. You can make it a reality; if you just keep pushing and keep trying, then eventually you'll reach your goal. And if that takes a few years, then that's great, but if it takes 10 or 20, then that's part of the process. - Naomi Osaka

Take up one idea. Make that one idea your life think of it, dream of it, live on that idea. Let the brain, muscles, nerves, every part of your body be full of that idea, and just leave every other idea alone. This is the way to success. - Swami Vivekananda

When a person can't find a deep sense of meaning, they distract themselves with pleasure. – Victor Franki

When you know what a man wants you know who he is and how to move him. - Petyr Baelish

My passion for mental health fuels my role as a beacon of strength and compassion. Through empathy and dedication, I inspire growth and healing. May the seeds of empowerment I sow blossom into resilience and self-discovery for other. - Felicia Pierce

. . .

Failure is a part of life. If you don't fail, you don't learn. If you don't learn, you'll never change. - Morgan Freeman

Happiness is a choice, not a result. Nothing will make you happy until you choose to be happy. No person will make you happy unless you decide to be. Your happiness will not come to you. It only come from you. - Ralph Marston

Hope - if you carry one thing throughout your entire life, let it be hope. Let be hope that better things are always ahead. Let it be hope that you can be through even the toughest of times. Let it be hope that you are stronger than any challenge that comes your way. Let it be hope that you are exactly where you are meant to be right now, and that you are on the path to where you are meant to be. Because during these times, hope will be the very thing that carries you through. - Nikki Banas

People are loyal to those who pay their wages. – Tommy Shelby

Success is not final; failure is not fatal. It is courage to continue that counts. - Wilson Churchill

Gentle reminder that you are doing your best and even though things have not been easy on you, you are still strong enough to make it through. Hold on yourself with kindness and love during this long season of strangeness and hurt and let go of everything that weighs heavy on your heart., that does not allow you to be who you are meant to become. - Dhiman

. . .

No matter how cool, talented, educated, or rich you are, how you treat people tells everything about you. Always remember integrity is everything. - Ravindra Kumar A

Self-control is strength. Calmness is mastery. You have to get to a point where your mood doesn't shift based on the insignificant actions of someone else. Don't allow others to correct the direction of your life. Don't allow your emotions to empower your intelligence. - Veronique Kelly

Self-Awareness mind helps you build on your strengths and improve on your weaknesses. – Peart Zhu

Love and friendship are exactly the same thing. Which is another way of saying that friendship is perhaps is the highest form of love in as much as love is the highest form of friendship. Think about when you have best friend you love them. Except instead of telling them that you love them you make them feel loved. You listen to them no matter what they have to say. You support them no matter what they're going through. It's like you want the best for them. Their happiness is yours and therefore, a true friend is someone who doubles your pleasures and divides your sorrows. Friendship is in fact a form of love and to have a best friend is therefore to have found a love for the rest of your life. - Julian de Medeiros

Maturity is when you stop asking people why they don't care or text you anymore. You just notice the change and accept it, no drama, no fights. You just walk away with a smile. – Morgan Freeman

Only a positive mind can move the world forward. – Peart Zhu

. . .

The more chances you give someone, the less respect they'll start to have for you. They'll begin to ignore the standards that you've set because they'll know another chance will always be given. They're not afraid to lose you because they know no matter what you won't walk away. They get comfortable with depending on your forgiveness. Never let a person get comfortable disrespecting you. -Trent Shelton

Success consists of going from failure to failure without loss of enthusiasm. - Winston Churchill

Worry is a total waste of time. It doesn't change anything. All it does is steal your joy and keep you busy doing nothing. - Denis Agaba

He's not perfect. You aren't either, and the two of you will never be perfect. But if he can make you laugh at least once, causes you to think twice, and if he admits to being human and making mistakes, hold onto him and give him the most you can. He isn't going to quote poetry, he's not thinking about you every moment, but he will give you a part of him that he knows you could break. Don't hurt him, don't change him, and don't expect for more than he can give. Don't analyze. Smile when he makes you happy, yell when he makes you mad, and miss him when he's not there. Love hard when there is love to be had. Because perfect guys don't exist, but there's always one guy that is perfect for you. - Bob Marley

Some people will only "love you" as much as they can use you. Their loyalty ends where the benefits stop. - Denis Agaba

. . .

You have to train your mind to be strong than your feelings or else you gone lose yourself. -Tyson

Do not lower your standards to keep people around you. Make them meet you at your level self-respect is power. - Will Smith

Forgive anyone who has caused you pain or harm. Keep in mind that forgiving is not for others. It is for you. Forgiving is not forgetting. It frees up your power, heals your body, mind and spirit. Forgiveness opens up a pathway to a new place of peace where you can persist despite what has happened to you. - Les Brown

Next time you're stressed, take a step back, inhale and laugh. Remember who you are and why you're here. You're never given anything in the world that you can't handle it. Be strong, be flexible, love yourself, and love others. Always remember, just keep moving forward. - Sharan Kaur

Get up in the morning and look at the world in a way that takes nothing for granted. Everything is phenomenal; everything is incredible; never treat life casually. To be spiritual is to be amazed. - Abraham Joshua Heschel

The scariest thought in the world is that someday I'll wake up and realize I've been sleepwalking through my life: under-appreciating the people I love, making the same hurtful mistakes over and over, a slave to neuroses, fear and the habitual. - George Saunders

. . .

Sometimes you climb out of bed in the morning and you think, I'm not going to make it, but you laugh inside-remembering all the times you've felt that way. - Charles Bukowski

Each day provides its own gifts. - Marcus Aurelius

So fine was the morning except for a streak of wind here and there that the sea and sky looked all one fabric, as if sails were stuck high up in the sky, or the clouds had dropped down into the sea. - Virginia Woolf

Before I leave the house, I say five things I love about myself, like 'You have really pretty eyes.' That way I can go out into the world with that little bit of extra confidence. - Jennifer Love Hewitt

The purpose of life is not to be happy. It is to be useful, to be honorable, to have it make some difference that you have lived well. - Ralph Waldo Emerson

Pause before judging. Pause before accusing. Pause before assuming. Pause whenever you're about to react harshly, and you'll avoid doing and saying things you will regret later. - Lori Deschene

The more chances you give someone, the less respect they'll start to have for you. They'll begin to ignore the standards that you've set because they'll know another chance will always be given. They're not afraid to lose you because they know no matter what you won't walk away. They get comfortable with depending on your forgiveness. Never let a person get comfortable disrespecting you. -Trent Shelton

Every struggle in your life has shaped you into the person you are today. Be thankful for the hard times, they can only make you stronger. - Denis Agaba

Forgive anyone who has caused you pain or harm. Keep in mind that forgiving is not for others. It is for you. Forgiving is not forgetting. It frees up your power, heals your body, mind and spirit. Forgiveness opens up a pathway to a new place of peace where you can persist despite what has happened to you. - Les Brown

Learning how to be calm when you're disrespected is a super power. - Denis Agaba

The moment when you first wake up in the morning is the most wonderful of the 24 hours. No matter how weary or dreary you may feel, you possess the certainty that, during the day that lies before you, absolutely anything may happen. And the fact that it practically always doesn't, matters not a jot. The possibility is always there. - Monica Baldwin

Challenge your limit, never miss an opportunity. – Alston Theodorus

Opportunity is the best captain of all endeavor. – Sophocles

. . .

The greatest opportunities today are to go into business for yourself as an entrepreneur. - Paul Zane Pilzer

You've got to wake up each day and understand what that day is about; you've got to have personal goals. Be flexible in getting to those goals, but if you do not have goals, you will not achieve them. - Cary Cohn

Your morning sets up the success of your day. So many people wake up and immediately check text messages, emails, and social media. I use my first hour awake for my morning routine of breakfast and meditation to prepare myself. - Caroline Ghosn

Your attitude is like a box of crayons that color your world. Constantly color your picture gray, and your picture will always be bleak. Try adding some bright colors to the picture by including humor, and your picture begins to lighten up. – Allen Klein

If you build army of 100 lions and their leader is a dog, in any fight, the lions will die like a dog. But if you build and army of 100 dogs and their leader is a lion, all dogs will fight as a lion. - Napoleon Bonaparte

Don't force yourself to fit in where you don't belong. -Tiffany M. Hart

The purpose of our lives is to be happy. - Dalai Lama

. . .

Feed your mind with positive thoughts, and attract great things into your life. - Kathy Nichols

The things you think about determining the quality of your mind. - Marcus Aurelius

The truth is confidence is not a personality trait at all. It's a skill. And a lot of extroverted people that you know are actually very insecure. And so, when you start to separate confidence not a matter of personality, but as a skill that you can acquire, because confidence is the ability to move in my opinion, from thought to action. - Mel Robbins

Leopard in the zoo is as powerful as leopard born in the jungle. But the leopard in the jungle has more respect because it knows how to hunt. – Sit Prasad Kamune

Every time you get upset at something ask yourself if you were to die tomorrow, was it worth wasting your time being angry. – Robert Tew.

Sometimes you just have to die a little inside in order to be reborn and rise again as a strong and wiser version of you. – Josh Loe

Greatness lies not in being strong, but in the right use of strength. – Henry Ward Beecher

·   ·   ·

I don't chase after people anymore. If they like spending time with me, they will do so. If mot, I'm content in my own company. – Barry M. Sherbal

If you focus on the hurt, you will continue to suffer. If you focus on the lesson, you will continue to grow. - Denis Agaba

Next time you're stressed, take a step back, inhale and laugh. Remember who you are and why you're here. You're never given anything in the world that you can't handle it. Be strong, be flexible, love yourself, and love others. Always remember, just keep moving forward. - Sharan Kaur

Sometimes life will kick you around, but sooner or later, you realize you're not a survivor. You're a warrior, and you're stronger than anything life throws your way. - Brooks Davis

I don't always learn my lesson. But when I do, you can bet I learned it the hardest way. – Robert de Niro

Even the nicest people have their limit. Don't push them too far and don't force to reach those limits because the nicest people can also be the scariest assholes once they've had enough. - Keanu Reeves

Don't judge. Nobody has it easy, everybody has problems. You never know what people are going through. So, before you start judging, criticizing or mocking others, remember everybody is fighting their own battle. - Denis Agaba

. . .

A true friend doesn't care if you're broke, upset, what you weigh, if your house is a mess, what car you drive, or if your family is filled with crazy people. They love you for who you are. - Denis Agaba

All birds find shelter during a rain. But Eagles avoid rain by flying above the Clouds. Problems are common, but attitude makes the difference. - Steven Kanumba

Do everything with a good heart and expect nothing in return and you will never be disappointed. - Denis Agaba

Never feel sad on losing anything in your life because whenever a tree loses its leaf, a new leaf is ready to take its place. - Peter B. Helland

Care about what other people think and you will always be their prisoner. - Lao Tzu

Smart people learn from everything and everyone. Average people from their experiences. Stupid people already have all the answers. - Socrates

You can only win when your mind is stronger than your emotions. - Denis Agaba

It's time to slow down and allow your body and mind rest. - Ludwig Van Beethov

. . .

The greatest weapon against stress is our ability to choose one thought over another. -William James.

Taking a break from someone will either make you realize how much you miss them, or how much peace you have without them. - Grizz

Being kind is very important. But most importantly, be kind to yourself. Because the true practice of love and kindness starts with self-love and self-kindness. - Ravindra Kumar A

Be strong, but not rude. Be kind, but not weak. Be bold, but not bully. Be humble, but not shy. Be confident, but to arrogant. -Nana Agyeman

It is not enough to be in the right place at the right time. You should also have an open mind at the right time. - Paul Erdős

Intelligence is a very valuable thing, in nit, my friend. And usually, it comes far too fucking late. -Alfie Solomons

My Suits Are on The House, Or the House Burns Down. – Tommy Shelby

Every man, he craves certainty. – Alfie Solomons

. . .

Lies travel faster than the truth. - Thomas Shelby

Never give power to the big man. -Alfie Solomons

There is no rest for me in this world. Perhaps in the next. – Tommy Shelby

Men always tell their troubles to a barmaid. - Grace

There's a part of me that is unfamiliar to myself. And I keep finding myself there. - Tommy Shelby

Rule one, you don't punch above your weight. - Polly Gray

That's funny, don't you think? A war about peace. -Tommy Shelby

In all the world the only thing that interests me is the truth. - Chester Campbell

Brave is going where no man has gone before. – Aunt Polly

Good taste is for people who can't afford sapphires. - Tommy Shelby

Men don't have the strategic intelligence to conduct a war between families. Men are less good at keeping secrets out of their lives. - Polly Gray

You strike when your enemy is weak. – Tommy Shelby

Killing a man affects the heart. - Chester Campbell

An agreement is not the same thing as an assurance. – Chester Campbell

To make sure your dog obeys you, you have to show it the stick once in a while. - Chester Campbell

We live somewhere between life and death, waiting to move on. And in the end, we accept it. We shake hands with devils, and we walk past them. -Aunt Polly

You don't get what you deserve, you get what you take. – Tommy Shelby

Sometimes beautiful things come into our lives out of nowhere. We can't always understand them, but we have to trust in them. I know you want to question everything, but sometimes it pays to just have a little faith. - Lauren Kate

Don't speak negative about yourself even as a joke. Your body doesn't know the difference. Words are Energy. Change the way you speak about yourself. And you can change your life. - Rybina Mughal

Never be ashamed of yourself. Be proud of who you are and don't worry about how others see you. - Kristen Butler

Stick with yourself, tolerant with others. – Marcus Aurelius

Once you figure out who you are and what you love about yourself, I think it all kind of falls into place. - Jennifer Aniston

I'm selfish, impatient and a little insecure. I make mistakes, I am out of control and at times hard to handle. But if you can't handle me at my worst, then you sure as hell don't deserve me at my best. - Marilyn Monro

If you tell the truth, you don't have to remember anything. - Mark Twain

In pubs sometimes people say things and sometimes it's the whisky talking. It's hard to tell which is which. - Tommy Shelby

Life is so much easier to deal with when you are dead. - Alfie Solomons

A man needs to prove he is better than me, rather than show me his birth certificate. – Tommy Shelby

. . .

Ambition for respectability doesn't make you a saint. – Father John Hughes

You don't have to see the whole staircase, just take the first step. - Martin Luther King Jr.

To be successful you must accept all challenges that come your way. You can't just accept the ones you like. - Mike Gafka

Opportunity is the best captain of all endeavors. - Sophocles

Courage is not having the strength to go on; it is going on when you don't have the strength. - Theodore Roosevelt

Be like the flower, turn your face to the sun. - Kahlil Gibran

The strength of a wall is neither greater nor less than the courage of the men who defend it. - Genghis Khan

If you aren't going all the way, why go at all? - Joe Namath

Each time we face a fear, we gain strength, courage, and confidence in the doing. - Wise Man

. . .

Most of our obstacles would melt away if, instead of cowering before them, we should make up our minds to walk boldly through them. - Orison Marden

It takes a great deal of courage to stand up to your enemies, but even more to stand up to your friends. - J.K. Rowling

When the student is ready, the teacher appears. When the student is truly ready, the teacher disappears. - Lao Tzu

No one has the right to judge you, because no one really knows what you have been through. They might hear the stories, but they didn't feel what you felt in your heart. - Keanu Reeves

People who know little are usually great talkers, while men who know much say little. - Jean Jacques Rousseau

In the end, it's not the years in your life that count. It's the life in your years. - Abraham Lincoln

The deepest sin against the human mind is to believe things without evidence. - Aldous Huxley

The goals of life are to live in agreement with nature. – Zeno

Mostly it is loss that teaches us about the worth of things. - Arthur Schopenhauer

. . .

If you don't like something, change it. If you can't change it, change your attitude. – Maya Angelou

Think of yourself as dead. You have lived your life. Now, take what is left and live it properly. – Marcus Aurelus

Experience is the teacher of all things. – Julius Caesar

When someone is properly grounded in life, they shouldn't have to look outside themselves for approval. - Epictetus

Those of you who are last will soon be first. And those of you who are downtrodden will rise. – Tommy Shelby

If you are going through hell, keep going. Why would you stop there? – Winston Churchill

Don't force your children into your ways, for they we're created for a time different from your own. – Plato

Don't worry about losing. If it is right, it happens. The main thing is not to hurry. Nothing good gets away. – John Steinbeck

Yesterday is history, tomorrow is a mystery, today is a gift of God, which is why we call it the present. - Bill Keane

. . .

I have not failed. I've just found 10,000 ways that won't work. - Thomas A. Edison

Absence makes the heart grow fonder. – Sextus Aurelius Propertius

Actions speak louder than words. – Mark Twain

Man conquers the world but conquering himself. – Zeno

All good things must come to an end. – Chaucer (1374) Proverb

A picture is worth a thousand words. – Fred Barnhart

A watched pot never boils. – Benjamin Franklin

Beggars can't be choosers. – John Heywood

Beauty is in the eye of the beholder. – Margaret Wolfe Hungerford

Better late than never. - Socrates

Birds of a feather flock together. – William Turner

. . .

Cleanliness is next to godliness. – John Wesley

Don't bite the hand that feeds you. – Greek poet Sappho

Don't count your chickens before they hatch. – Thomas Howell (1570) Proverb

Don't judge a book by its cover. – George Elliot (1860)

Don't put all of your eggs in one basket. – Thomas Howell (1570)

Don't put off until tomorrow what you can do today. – Benjamin Franklin

Stay focused and don't try to do too many things at once. Care about execution quality. – Sam Altman.

Easy come, easy go. - Ancient Chinese 400 B.C Proverb

Fortune favors the bold. – Terence s Roman playwright (161 BC) Proverb

God helps those who help themselves. – Aesop's Fables

. . .

Good things come to those who wait. – Abraham Lincoln Proverb

Honesty is the best policy. – Benjamin Franklin (1700s) Proverb

Hope for the best, prepare for the worst. – Gary Busey Proverb

If it ain't broke, don't fix it. – Thomas Bertram Lance

If you can't beat them, join them. - Aristotle

If you play with fire, you'll get burned. – Bam Bam Bigelow

If you want a thing done well, do it yourself. – Napoleon Bonaparte

Keep your friends close, and your enemies closer. – Sun Tzu

Knowledge is power. – Francis Beacon (1561-1626) Proverb

Laughter is the best medicine. – The Book of Proverbs in the Old Testament

No man is an island. – John Donne (17th Century) Proverb

.   .   .

People who live in glass houses should not throw stones. – Geoffrey Chaucer's Troilus and Criseyde (1385) Proverb

Practice makes perfect. – Bruce Lee

The early bird gets the worm. – William Camden (1605)

The enemy of my enemy is my friend. – Imam Ali in the book Nahj-albalaga Proverb

The grass is always greener on the other side. – Publius Ovidius Naso (Ovid 43 BC -17 AD) Proverb

The pen is mightier than the sword. – Edward Bulwer Lytton (1839) Proverb

There is no place like home. – Judy Garland as Dorothy in the 1939 classic film, "The Wizard of Oz Proverb.

There is no such thing as a free lunch. - Robert Heinlein (1949) Proverb

There is no time like the present. – John Trusler (1970) Proverb

The squeaky wheel gets the grease. – John Billings (1818-1885) Proverb

. . .

You have brains in your head. You have feet in your shoes. You can steer yourself any direction you choose. You're on your own. And you know what you know. And YOU are the one who'll decide where to go. - Dr. Seuss

Life isn't about finding yourself. Life is about creating yourself. - George Bernard Shaw

Success is not final; failure is not fatal: it is the courage to continue that counts. - Winston S. Churchill

A wise man was asked, "What is anger?" He gave a beautiful answer, "It is a punishment you give to yourself, for somebody else's mistakes." - Patricia Ophelia

The one who keeps causing you pain can never be your peace. - Tommy Shelby

A seed grows with No Sound, but a tree falls with huge noise. Destruction has Noise, but Creation is Quiet. This is the power of silence. Grow Silently. - Buddha

A man may fail many times, but he isn't a failure until he begins to blame somebody's else. - John Burroughs

. . .

If you don't know the guy on the other side of the world, love him anyway because he's just like you. He has the same dreams, the same hopes and fears. It's one world, pal. We're all neighbors. - Frank Sinatra

He who is healthy, has hope, and who has hope, has everything. - Thomas Carlyle

The deepest pain I ever felt was denying my own feelings to make everyone else comfortable. - Nicole Lyons

Everyday mindfulness: Change your life by living in the present. - Jennifer Brooks

I don't know where I'm going from here, but I promise it won't be boring. - David Bowie

You don't have to be perfect to help people. All you have to be is real. - Trent Shelton

You practice and you get better, It's very simple. – Philip Glass

Age is not the enemy. Stagnation is the enemy. - Twila Tharp Dancer

The bad news is time flies. The good news is you're the pilot. - Michael Altshules

. . .

If you give your trust to a person who does not deserve it, you actually give him the power to destroy you. - Khaled Saad

Open and honest communication is not only a necessary part of a successful marriage, but any relationship. - Sad Tasleem

Development is about transforming the lives of people, not just transforming economies. - Joseph E. Stiglitz

A person who never made a mistake, never tried anything new. - Albert Einstein

Every man is born an original, but sadly most men die copies. - Abraham Lincoln

Believe in yourself and all that you are. Know that there is something inside you that is greater than any obstacle. - Christian D. Larson

I'm Just an Extreme Example of What a Working-Class Man Can Achieve. – Tommy Shelby

No matter how many mistakes you make or how you progress, you are still way of everyone who isn't trying. - Tony Robbins

It is our attitude at the beginning of a difficult task which more than anything else will affect its successful outcome. - William James

. . .

If money is your hope for independence, you will never have it. The only real security that a man will have in this world is a reserve of knowledge, experience, and ability. - Henry Ford

An optimist stays up until midnight to see the New Year in. A pessimist stays up to make sure the old year leaves. - William E. Vangham

Year's end is neither an end nor a beginning, but a going on. - Hal Borland

To create the life of your dreams, the time has come to love you. Focus on your joy. Do all the things that make you feel good. Love you inside and out. Everything will change in your life, when you chance the inside of you. Allow the Universe to give you every good thing you deserve by being a magnet to them all. To be a magnet for every single thing you deserve you must be a Brooks Davis magnet pf love. - Rhonda Byrne

In the end, when it's all over, all that matters is what you've done. – Alexander The Great

For those who make the rules, there are no rules. - Tommy Shelby

The mind is not a vessel to be filled but a fire to be kindled. - Plutarch

. . .

I don't need a knife to stop me from telling secrets given in confidence. It is a matter of honor. – Esme Shelby

Do you know what's the saddest thing about betrayal? It Never comes from your enemy. - Tommy Shelby

Of all the disorders in the soul, envy is the only one no one confesses to. - Plutarch

Ask yourself at every moment is this necessary? - Marcus Aurelius

If a man knows not to which port he sails, no winds is favorable. – Seneca

Man, only likes to count his troubles, he doesn't calculate his happiness. – Dostoevsky

Remember that: You'll never be criticized by someone who is doing more than you. You'll always be criticized by someone doing less. - Denzel Washington

You should set goals beyond your reach so you always have something to live for. - Ted Turner

It must be borne in mind that the tragedy of life doesn't lie in not reaching your goal. The tragedy lies in having no goals to reach. - Benjamin E. Mays

. . .

People thinking I'm going to fall; they start behaving in a different way around you. – Tommy Shelby

When it is obvious that the goals cannot be reached, don't adjust the goals, adjust the action steps. - Confucius

Entrepreneurial leadership requires the ability to move quickly when opportunity presents itself. – Brian Tracy

There's nothing better than achieving your goals, whatever they might be - Paloma Faith

You cannot expect to achieve new goals or move beyond your present circumstances unless you change. - Les Brown

To make no mistakes is not in the power of man; but from their errors and mistakes the wise and good learn wisdom for the future. - Plutarch

Without some goals and some efforts to reach it, no man can live. - John Dewey

Set realistic goals, keep re-evaluating, and be consistent. - Venus Williams

. . .

Goals are not only absolutely necessary to motivate us. They are essential to really keep us alive. - Robery H. Schuller

Set realistic goals, keep re-evaluating, and be consistent. - Ginni Rometti

It's an up and down thing, the human goals, because the human is always an explorer, an adventurist. - Cesar Millan

If you set your goals ridiculously high and it's a failure, you will fail above everyone else's success. - James Cameron

I am constantly re-evaluating my goals and trying to strike items from my to-do list that aren't critical. - Aisha Tyler

People are not disturbed by things, but by the views they take of them. – Epictetus

I'm not crazy, I'm just not like you. – David Goggins

You can change what you do, but you can't change what you want. - Thomas Shelby

I don't need a friend who changes when I change and who nods when I nod; my shadow does that much better. - Plutarch

. . .

You need lofty goals. Then cement it with a great work ethic. - Jerry West

The real destroyer of the liberties of the people is he who spreads among them bounties, donations and benefits. - Plutarch

All successful people have a goal. No one can get anywhere unless he knows where he wants to go and what he wants to be or do. - Norman Vincent Peale

Where are the people who don't have goals headed? Those 97 per cent end up working for the three percent. - Shiv Khera

I like to tell young people to work hard for your goals and live in the moment. - Nadia Comaneci

People often say I have so much energy, that I never stop; but that's what it takes to accomplish your goals. - Curtis Jackson

My personal goals are to be happy, healthy and to be surrounded by loved ones. - Kiana Tom

To find fault is easy; to do better may be difficult. - Plutarch

It's harder to stay on top than it is to make the climb. Continue to seek new goals. - Pat Summitt

. . .

If you want to live a happy life, tie it to a goal, not to people or things. – Albert Einstein

One way to keep momentum going is to have constantly greater goals. – Michael Korda

The greater danger for most of us isn't that our aim is too high and miss it, but that it is too low and we reach it. - Michelangelo

Goals are the fuel in the furnace of achievement. - Brian Tracy

I am always more interested in what I am about to do than what I have already done. – Rachel Carson

Setting goals is the first step in turning the invisible into the visible. – Tony Robbins

If a goal is worth having, it's worth blocking out the time in your day-to-day life necessary to achieve it. - Jill Koenig

In between goals is a thing called life, that has to be lived and enjoyed. - Sid Caeser

You can always find a solution if you try hard enough. - Lori Greiner

The going is the goal. - Horace Kallen.

. . .

A good goal is like a strenuous exercise, it makes you stretch. - Mary Kay Ash

Knowing is not enough; we must apply. Willing is not enough; we must do. - Johann Wolfgang von Goethe

There are only two rules for being successful. One, figure out exactly what you want to do, and two, do it. - Mario Cuomo

You are stepping into a world you don't understand. -Tommy Shelby

What you get by achieving your goals is not as important as what you become by achieving your goals. – Henry David Thoreau

Life can be pulled by goals just as surely as it can be pushed by drives. - Viktor Frankl

he great glorious masterpiece of man is to know how to live with purpose. - Michel de Montaigne

Intention without action is an insult to those who expect the best from you. - Andy Andrews

. . .

A goal is not always meant to be reached; it often serves simply as something to aim at. - Bruce Lee

You cannot change your destination overnight, but you can change your direction overnight. - Jim Rohn

Discipline is the bridge between goals and accomplishment. - Jim Rohn

To reach a port, we must sail, sail, not tie at anchor, sail, not drift. - Franklin Roosevelt

Be practical as well as generous in your ideals. Keep your eyes on the stars, but remember to keep your feet on the ground. - Theodore Roosevelt

The greatest mistake you can make in life is to continually be afraid you will make one. - Elbert Hubbard

Do not let what you cannot do interfere with what you can do. - John Wooden

You are never too old to set a new goal or to dream a new dream. - C.S. Lewis

If we have a goal and a plan, and are willing to take risks and mistakes and work as team, we can choose to do the hard thing. - Scott Kelly

Never give up. Today is hard, tomorrow will be worse, but the day after tomorrow will be sunshine. - Jack Ma

What we achieve inwardly will change outer reality. - Plutarch

We think, mistakenly, that success is the result of the amount of time we put in at work, instead of the quality of time we put in. - Arianna Huffington

You can't be that kid standing at the top of the waterslide, overthinking it. You have to go down the chute. - Tina Fey

If something is important enough, even if the odds are against you, you should still do it. - Elon Musk

A goal without a timeline is just a dream. - Robert Herjavec

It always seems impossible until it's done. - Nelson Mandela

Success consists of going from failure to failure without loss of enthusiasm. - Winston Churchill

. . .

You have to be able to get up and dust yourself off and always be going forward. - Rita Moreno

You'll never find time for anything. If you want time, you must make it. – Charles Buxton

Hustling is putting every minute and all your effort into achieving the goal at hand. Every minute needs to count. – Gary Vaynerchuk

A year from now you may wish you had started today. – Karen Lamb

Dream your own dreams, achieve your own goals. Your journey is your own and unique. – Roy T. Bennett

It's better to be at the bottom of the ladder you want to climb than at the top of the one you don't. – Stephen Kellogg

A goal is a dream with a deadline. – Napoleon Hill

Things won are done; joy's soul lies in the doing. – William Shakespeare

Every ceiling, when reached, becomes a floor, upon which one walks as a matter of course and prescriptive right. – Aldous Huxley

. . .

Our goals can only be reached through a vehicle of a plan, in which we must fervently believe, and upon which we must vigorously act. There is no other route to success. – Pablo Picasso

A river cuts through rock, no because of its power, but because of its persistence. – JamesN. Walkins

The virtue lies in the struggle, not in the prize. – Richard Monckton Milnes

A good archer is known not by his arrows but by his aim. – Thomas Fuller

Think little goals and expect little achievements. Think big goals and win big success. - David Joseph Schwartz

No desired achievement is gained without any goal setting. - Wayne Chirisa

I love the challenge of starting at zero every day and seeing how much I can accomplish. - Martha Stewart

The great secret about goals and visions is not the future they describe, but the change in the present they engender. - David Allen

The way to achieve your goals is step by step, you just need to build enough track, to be ahead of the train. - John Milton Lawrence

. . .

The only goals you don't achieve in life are the goals you don't set. - Matt Fox

If you really look closely, most overnight successes took a long time. - Steve Jobs

It doesn't matter how many times you fail. You only have to be right once and then everyone can tell you that you are an overnight success. - Mark Cuban

All our dreams can come true, if we have the courage to pursue them. - Walt Disney

Don't worry about being successful but work toward being significant and the success will naturally follow. – Oprah Winfrey

Goals are dreams brought to life. – Amy Leigh Mercree

Wish it. Plan it. Do it. – Jaipal Singh

You know that one thing you've always dreamed about? Write it down. Then take the first step. Today. – Petra Poje

One person may not, whereas another person will. Your job is to find a person who will help you reach your goal. – Germany Kent

. . .

A birthday is a time to reflect on the year gone by, but to also set your goals for the upcoming year. - Catherine Pulsifer

The goal is not to be better than the other man, but your previous self. - Dalai Lama

Any of us carry baggage from the past that hinders our ability to fight for the things we want in life, our goals, our dreams. – Les Brown

Motivation is what drives a person to move forward and put action towards making their goals happen. – Brian Cagneey

Motivation is interwoven with the goals you make and the habits you form in order to achieve them. - Matthew Lewis Browne

We must share our dreams with people who will see us working toward and accomplishing our goals. Be encouraged by people who say, "How about trying it this way? – David DeNotaris

The best way to approach a goal is to first break it down into very small bite size steps. Each one of these steps should lead logically to the next step to be completed in a linear order. – Byron Pulsifer

You can accomplish whatever your mind can see! - Catherine Pulsifer

. . .

The main thing to keep in mind is that there can be many sets of small goals involved in working up to your final and ultimate goal. - Ben Johnson

Empowerment involves analyzing your own life and believing that you are able to reach realistic goals. - Poppy Fingley

The goal you set must be challenging. At the same time, it should be realistic and attainable, not impossible to reach. It should be challenging enough to make you stretch, but not so far that you break. - Rick Hansen

Goals can change from time to time but then remember to focus on your priorities. - Roger Collmar

Goals produce focus. Without a goal, there is no reason to focus on anything. Think of a goal as a target. - Bill Price

Without a goal, you will continue creating yourself in the manner you have been doing it so far. And obtaining the same expected results, more often, unconsciously. - Helena Angel

While working on completing your goal, you may encounter possible setbacks. Instead of beating yourself up, look at them as opportunities to learn and grow. - Kyle Nussen

. . .

The key to thriving with accomplishing any goal would be dependent on working with dedication, yet lots of people do not interpret just how important it really is. - Sarfraz Sohail

Any unforeseen challenges that crop up are only there to test your resolve on your way to ultimate success in reaching your goal." - Byron Pulsifer

Making sure our goals are properly aligned with our passions only makes sense. - Josh Hinds

Without any goal, it's as if you are only doing things in random. - Ryan Cooper

Goals are like a map. They help us determine where we want to end up, and give us personal direction on which to focus our energy. - Catherine Pulsifer

By having big goals and pushing yourself towards them you will have a lot more energy because you know exactly what you're doing and what you're doing it for. - Troy Foster

If you want to do something and you have a goal, do it, don't wait, because your channel might change sometime soon and quite unexpectedly. - Sean Swarner

Productivity depends on executing important tasks in line with your goals. - Romuald Andrade

. . .

If you want to achieve your goal, the strategy you are using need not be clever or original but it should bring results. - Andrii Sedniev

Basically, being in a team is an amalgamation of different things that have a common intention of meeting the assigned goal. - Derek Stanzma

Set goals and focus on completing one goal at a time. - K. Collins

Once you know specifically what you're aiming for, you'll find that you can muster up enthusiasm for your goal more easily. - AJ Winters

Set your goals high, and don't stop till you get there. – Bo Jackson

Do not speak of your happiness to one less fortunate than yourself. - Plutarch

Go out into the world with your passion and love for what you do, and just never give up. - Dianne Reeve

Sometimes life will kick you around, but sooner or later, you realize you're not a survivor. You're a warrior, and you're stronger than anything life throws your way. - Brooks Davis

. . .

I've found that the first thirty minutes of my day have the biggest impact on how I feel for the rest of my waking hours. – Molli Sullivan

For many years, my morning routine was a result of how other people expected me to show up. I was overwhelmed and off-center because I was ignoring the messages my body was sending me. – Amber Rae

It is never too late to be what you might have been. – George Eliot

Either write something worth reading or do something worth writing. – Benjamin Franklin

Your imagination is your preview of life's coming attractions. – Albert Einstein

There's always a sunrise and always a sunset and it's up to you to choose to be there for it, said my mother. 'Put yourself in the way of beauty. - Cheryl Strayed

You can only come to the morning through the shadows. - J.R.R. Tolkien

If the world were merely seductive, that would be easy. If it were merely challenging, that would be no problem. But I arise in the morning torn between a desire to improve the world and a desire to enjoy the world. This makes it hard to plan the day. - E.B. White

. . .

Those who dream by night in the dusty recesses of their minds wake up in the day to find it was vanity, but the dreamers of the day are dangerous men, for they may act their dreams with open eyes, to make it possible. - T.E. Lawrence

The day will be what you make it, so rise, like the sun, and burn. - William C. Hannan

Someday is not a day of the week. – Denise Brennan-Nelson

True terror is to wake up one morning and discover that your high school class is running the country. - Kurt Vonnegut

Choose what is best, and habit will make it pleasant and easy. - Plutarch

It isn't as bad as you sometimes think it is. It all works out. Don't worry. I say that to myself every morning. - Gordon B. Kinkley

When one begins to turn in bed, it is time to get up. – Arthur Wellesley

There is no sunrise so beautiful that it is worth waking me up to see it. - Mindy Kaling

. . .

Given another shot at life, I would seize every minute of it, look at it and really see it, try it on, live it, exhaust it and never give that minute back until there was nothing left of it. - Erma Bombeck

If you want to make your dreams, come true, the first thing you have to do is wake up. – J.M. Power

Clear, written goals have a wonderful effect on your thinking. They motivate you and galvanize you into action. They stimulate your creativity, release your energy, and help you to overcome procrastination as much as any other factor. – Brian Tracy

A good plan today is better than a perfect plan tomorrow. – George S. Patton

Don't judge each day by the harvest you reap but by the seeds that you plant. - Robert Louis Stevenson

Being defeated is often a temporary condition. Giving up is what makes it permanent. - Marilyn Vos Savant

Half of life is lost in charming others. The other half is lost in going through anxieties caused by others. Leave this play, you have played enough. - Rumi

There comes a point when you have to realize that you'll never good enough for some people. The question is, is that your problem or theirs? - Joey Ferrari

. . .

Choose not act on an angry impulse and to feel the pain that lies beneath is a very courageous thing to do. - Gary Zukav

You only live once, but if you do it right, once is enough. - Mar West

The key is to keep company only with people who uplift you, whose presence calls forth your best. - Epictetus

Remember no one can make you feel inferior without your consent. - Eleanor Roosevelt

Your worth consists in what you are and not in what you have. - Thomas Edison

Wise men speak because they have something to say; fools speak because they have to say something. - Socrates

The only true wisdom is knowing that you know nothing. - Plato
     Be a first-rate version of yourself, not a second-rate version of someone else. - Judy Garland

Be strong enough to stand alone, be yourself enough to stand apart, but be wise enough to stand together. - Native American Heritage

. . .

No one can escape death and unhappiness. If people expect only happiness in life, they will be disappointed. - Heart of Buddhism

Everybody isn't your friend. Just because they hand around you and laugh with you doesn't mean they are your friends. At the end of the day, real situations expose fake people, so pay attention. - Namasimeivan

A wise man said: "Don't seek revenge. The rotten fruits will fall by themselves. - Peter Nashukury

A woman can forget a man who broke her heart, but she never forgets the man who gathered the broken pieces, healed her soul, and made her smile again. Be that man in a woman 's life. - Natalie Taylor

Let me tell you a secret. No one does when they begin. Ideas don't come out fully formed. They only become clear as you work on them. You just have get started. - Zuckerberg

One of the happiest moments in life is when you find the courage to let of what you cannot change. - John David Keys

An imbalance between rich and poor is the oldest and most fatal ailment of all republics. - Plutarch

If you stay in your comfort zone, that's where you will fail. You will fail in your comfort zone. Success is not a comfortable procedure. It is very uncomfortable thing to attempt. So, you got to get comfortable being uncomfortable if you ever wanna be successful. Start putting some pressure on, put some pressure on yourself. - Steve Harvey

Life is a circle of happiness, sadness, hard times, and good times. If you are going through hard times, faith that good times are on the way. - Buddha

The man who removes a mountain begins by carrying away small stones. - Confucius

You will always see children fighting for inheritance, but you will never see them fighting to take care their sick parents. - Michael Jackson

Top trying to calm the storm. Calm yourself, the storm will pass. - Harvey Bullock

I hope you find the courage to start again. I hope even if you struggle to find your Stupid is knowing the truth, seeing the truth, but still believing the lies. - Morgan Freeman

When a bird is alive, it eats ants. When the bird is dead, ants eat the bird, Time and circumstances can change at any time. Don't devalue or hurt anyone in life, you may be powerful today, but remember, time is more powerful than you. - Rio Rel

. . .

Generosity is the vanity of giving. - La Rochefoucauld

Fearful is the seductive power of generosity. - Bertlt Brecht

May we cherish every moment of this fragile life. We are not promised tomorrow. Life is a gift; may we always see as much. - Sharon Seababy

To be successful you must accept all challenges that come your way. You can't just accept the ones you like. - Mike Gafka

Happiness is not something ready-made. It comes from your own actions. - Dalai Lama

Don't tell people what you're going to do. Do it and shock them. And after shocking them, stay silent. Move onto your next project. Keep shocking keep enjoying. – Bezos

One great lesson I learned from my life. There is no market for your emotions, so never advertise your feelings, just show your attitude. - Dennis Agaba

It's time to slow down and allow your body and mind rest. - Ludwig Van Beethov

You can forgive some people without welcoming them back into your life. Apology accepted; access denied. - Milly Stone.

. . .

The purpose of our lives is to be happy. - Dalai Lama

Life is what happens when you're busy making other plans. - John Lennon

Get busy living or get busy dying. - Stephen King

You only live once, but if you do it right, once is enough. - Mae West

Many of life's failures are people who did not realize how close they were to success when they gave up. - Thomas A. Edison

If you want to live a happy life, tie it to a goal, not to people or things. - Albert Einstein

Nothing can dim the light that shines from within. - Maya Angelou

Never expect to get what you give. Not everyone has a heart like you. - Lian Neeson

The measure of a man is the way he bears up under misfortune. - Plutarch

. . .

People will come and go in life, but the person in the mirror will be there forever. So be good to yourself. - Matilda A Buer Amon

Never be ashamed of yourself. Be proud of who you are and don't worry about how others see you. - Kristen Butler

The purpose of life is not to be happy. It is to be useful, to be honorable, to have it make some difference that you have lived well. - Ralph Waldo Emerson

Sometimes you find exactly what you're were looking for before you even realized you were looking for it. Stay open. Stay positive. Things can change overnight. - Doe Zantamata

The abuse of buying and selling votes crept in and money began to play an important part in determining elections. Later on, this process of corruption spread to the law courts. And then to the army, and finally the Republic was subjected to the rule of emperors. - Plutarch

Never let the fear of striking out keep you from playing the game. - Babe Ruth

Money and success don't change people; they merely amplify what is already there. - Will Smith

Yesterday, I was clever, so I wanted to change the world. Today, I'm wise enough, so I'm changing myself. - Rumi

. . .

Respect yourself and others will respect you. - Confucius

No, we don't always get what we want. But consider this: There are people who will never have what you have right now. - Denis Agaba

If you allow people to make more withdrawals than deposits in your life, you will be out of balance and it the negative. Know when to close the account. - Koko

Every bad situation in life has something positive. Even a dead clock shows correct time twice day. - Barack Obama

Life has knocked me down a few times. It has shown me things I never wanted to see. I have experienced sadness and failures. But one thing for sure I always get up. - Scott Calum

Reality of Life – When you give importance to people, they think you are always free, but they don't understand that you make yourself available for them. - Reder B. Helland

Stop being perfect because obsessing over being perfect stops you from growing. - Brad Pitt

Only you and you alone can change your situation. Don't blame it on others or anyone. - Leonardo DiCaprio

. . .

To win big you sometimes have to take big risks. - Bill Gates

You must fail a hundred times to succeed once. - Sylvester Stallone

Don't worry about hard times, because some of the greatest things we have come from trials in our life. - Denis Agaba

Sun is single. Moon is single. I am also single. That means all precious things are single. - Zubair Macalin

Confidence and hard work are the best medicine to kill the disease called failure. It will make you a successful person. - Ibra Kadbrah

The birds fine find in the rain. But Eagle avoid drain flying above the Clouds. Problems are common, but attitude makes the difference. – Dr. Abdul Kalam

It does not matter how slowly you go so long as you do not stop. - Confucius

If you want to shine like a sun, first burn like a sun. - Dr. Abdul Kalam

Don't take rest after your first victory because if you fail in second, more lips are waiting to say your first victory was just luck. - Dr. Abdul Kalam

. . .

Don't read success stories, you will only get a message. Read failure stories, you will get some ideas to get success. - Dr. Abdul Kalam

Success is when your signature becomes an Autograph. - Ibra Kadbrah

The man who asks question is a fool for a minute. The man who does not is a fool for life. - Confucius

Sometime people don't want to hear the truth. Because they don't want their illusions destroyed. - Nietzche

People shouldn't have many friends. Because you'll get tired of getting knives out of your back. - Epictetus

Small minded people blame others. Average people blame themselves. The wise see all blame as foolishness. - Epictetus

He who is not happy with little, will never be happy with much. - Epictetus

There is only one way to happiness and that is o cease worrying about things which are beyond our power or our will. - Epictetus

People who wonder if the glass is half empty or full, miss the point. The glass is refillable. - Simon Sinek

. . .

If you always defend your children mistake, one day you will hire a lawyer to defend their crime. Discipline is not child abuse. - Byamukama Stephen

From the errors of others, a wise man corrects his own. - Publilius Syrus

It does not matter how slowly you go as long as you do not stop. - Confucius

The man who chases two rabbits, catches neither. - Confucius

Take care of your body as if you live forever and take care of your soul as if you were going to die tomorrow. - Saint Augustine

Education is the most powerful weapon which you can use to change the world. - Nelson Mandela

If you're always trying to be normal, you will never know how amazing you can be. - Maya Angelou

You may not control all the events that's happen to you, but you can decide not to be reduced by them. Try to be a rainbow in someone else's cloud. Do not complain. Make every effort to change things you do not like. If you cannot make a change, change the way you have been thinking. You might find a new solution. - Maya Angelou

. . .

Believe in yourself and all that you are know that there is something inside of you that is greater than any obstacle. - Christian D Larson

Never expect to get what you give, not everyone has a heart like you. - Lian Neeson

I found the key to happiness, stay away from idiots. - Morgan Freeman

Doing the best all this moment puts you in the best place for the next moment. - Oprah Winprey

It does not matter how slowly you go as long as you do not stop. - Confucius

There is no key to happiness. The door is always open. - Mother Teresa

If you hate a person, then you're defeated by them. - Confucius

The be trusted is a greater compliment than being loved. - Leo Tolstoy

Raise your words, not voice. It's rain that grows flowers, not thunder. - Rumi

. . .

If you are depressed, you are living in the past. If you are anxious, you are living in the future. If you are at peace, you are living in the present. - Lao Tzu

Don't change so people will like you. Be yourself and the right people will love the real you. - Helen Barry

Soft hearted people know what people did to them. But they forgive again and again because they have beautiful hearts. - Helen Barry

Waking up to see another day is a blessing. Don't take it for granted. Make it count and be happy that you're alive. - Helen Barry

Your worth is not validated by the opinion of another. You have always been whole, enough and worthy of love. - Helen Barry

Life is too short to worry about what others say or think about you. So just enjoy life, have fun and give them something to talk about. - Helen Barry

At the end of the day what really matters is that your loved ones are well, you've done your best and that you're thankful for all you have. - Helen Barry

When you truly don't care what anyone thinks of you, you have reached a dangerously awesome level of freedom. - Helen Barry

. . .

I don't how can you deal with someone you can't trust? If the wagon has no axle, how can you ride it? - Confucius

Putting yourself first doesn't mean you don't care about others. It means you're smart enough to know you can't help others if you don't help yourself first. - Helen Barry

Success. Liking yourself. Liking what you do. Liking how you do it. - Maya Angelou

The less you respond to rude, critical, argumentative people, the more peaceful your life will become. - Mandy Hale

People will gossip no matter how hard you try to avoid it; make something great out of your life while the others waste their life gossip about yours. - Helen Barry

People will forget what you said, people will forget what you did, but people will never forget how you made them feel. - Maya Angelou

Don't judge me by my successes, judge me by how many times I felt down and got back up again. - Nelson Mandela

Everything will happen for you all of sudden and you'll be thankful you didn't give up. Believe that. - Vybe Source

. . .

Unconditional love = stress free life. Only those receive or give can understand this equation. - Balroop Singh

Don't carry your mistakes around you. Instead, place them under your feet and use them as stepping stones. Never regret. If it's good, it's wonderful. If it's bad it's am experience. - Dennis Agaba

Leadership is the ability to get extraordinary achievement from ordinary people. – Brian Tracy

The biggest coward is a man who awakens a woman's love with no intention of loving her. - Bod Marley

What's done is done. What's gone is gone. One of life's lessons is always moving on. It's ok to look back and think of fond memories but keep moving forward. - Denis Agaba

Don't let yourself be controlled by three things: people, money or past experiences. - Dennis Agaba

Don't let people make you feel bad or guilty for living your life. It is your life. Live it the way you want. - Lajian

Never judge people who have little to nothing, as one day you may find yourself having nothing at all. Always respect one another no matter what. Never look down on anyone. - Denis Agaba

. . .

The first person you think of in the morning, or last person you think of at night, is either the cause of your happiness or your pain. - Dorothy Mwari

Smile and let everyone know that today, you're a lot stronger than you were yesterday. - Drake

Some people want it to happen, some wish it would happen, others make it happen. - Michael Jordan

Don't criticize your neighbor's roof for a neighbor's roof of snow when your door is not clean. - Confucius

The most difficult thing is the decision to act, the rest is merely tenacity. - Amelia Earhart

If you hear a voice within you say, 'You cannot paint,' then by all means paint, and that voice will be silenced. - Vincent Van Gogh

There is always light. If only we're brave enough to see it. If only we're brave enough to be it. - Amanda Gorman

You're braver than you believe, stronger than you seem, and smarter than you think. - A.A. Milne

However difficult life may seem, there is always something you can do and succeed at. - Stephen Hawking

. . .

The two most important days in your life are the day you are born and the day you figure out why. - Mark Twain

I learned a long ago that there is something worse than missing the goal, and that's not pulling the trigger. - Mia Hamm

Be thankful for what you have; you'll end up having more. If you concentrate on what you don't have, you will never, ever have enough. - Oprah Winfrey

Difficulties in your life do not come to destroy you. But to help you realize your hidden potential and power. Let difficulties know that you too are difficult. - A.P.J. Abdul Kalamn

Sometimes the strongest among us are the one who smile through silent pain, cry behind closed doors, and fight battles nobody knows about. - John David

Never make a permanent decision based on a temporary emotion. - Unknown

Forgive people in your life, even those who are not sorry for their actions. Holding on the anger only hurts you, not them. - Lajian

Sometimes what you want isn't always what you get, but in the end what you get is so much better than what you wanted. - John David Keys

Don't compare your life to others. There's no comparison between the sun and the moon. They shine when it's their time. - Najjenba Jovia

Respect Yourself- Removing toxic people from your life doesn't mean that you hate them. It simply means that you respect yourself. - Jordan Lane

Take care of your body as if you live forever; and take care of your soul as if you were going to die tomorrow. - Saint Augustine

No one can destroy iron, but its own rust can, likewise no one can destroy a person, but his own mindset can. - Najjemba Jovia

If you aren't going all the way, why go at all? - Joe Namath

Most of our obstacles would melt away if, instead of cowering before them, we should make up our minds to walk boldly through them. - Orison Marden

It takes a great deal of courage to stand up to your enemies, but even more to stand up to your friends. - J.K. Rowling

. . .

Success is not final; failure is not fatal. It is the courage to continue that counts. - Winston Churchill

The strength of a wall is neither greater nor less than the courage of the men who defend it. - Genghis Khan

Be like a flower, turn your face to the sun. - Kahlil Gibran

Opportunity is the best captain of all endeavor. - Sophocles

Courage is not having the strength to go on, it is going on when you don't have the strength. - Theodore Roosvelt

To see the right and not to do it is cowardice. - Confucius

Sometimes you feel tired of your situation, but always remember, that's not permanent. Don't lose hope. - Milly Stone

When life gives you a hundred reasons to break down and cry, show life that you have a million reasons to smile and laugh, Stay strong. - George Mintah

Opportunity is the best captain of all endeavor. - Sophocles

If you ever notice, the people who often end up alone are those who love to much, care too much and are too gentle and kind. - Keanu Reeves

Life is never easy. Whatever comes to you, be firm and the bravest you can be. It's okay to cry, be upset and let it out, but never lose hope. Never give up. In times of confusion and in times when you're running out of choices, be reminded of one thing: Sincere Prayer does change things. - George Mintah

Sometimes you just have to play the role of a fool to fool the fool who thinks they are fooling you. - Vandell Andreou

Always remember: Never be too much available for someone otherwise you will lose your importance. - Larry Josh

Ungrateful people complain about the one thing you did wrong, instead of being thankful for the hundreds of things you have done for them. - George Mintah

Time decides who you meet in your life. Heart decides what you want in your life. But your behavior decides who will stay in your life. - Brin Adams

When you forgive, you in no way change the past, but you sure do change the future. - Bernard Meltzer

Discipline is doing what needs to be done, even if you don't want to do it. - Greek Proverb

. . .

Happiness is not something readymade. It comes from your own actions. - Dalai Lama

When you feel powerless, that's because you stopped listening to your heart, that's where the power comes from. - Gianni Crow

Don't speak negative about yourself even as a joke. Your body doesn't know the difference. Words are Energy. Change the way you speak about yourself. And you can change your life. - Rybina Mughal

You make a choice: continue living your life feeling muddled in this abyss of self-misunderstanding, or you find your identity independent of it. You draw your own box. - Duchess Meghan

May love and light shine through your day. - Helen Barry

When the wrong people leave your life, the right things start happening. - Helen Barry

An unexamined life is not worth living. - Socrates

Don't let the behavior of others destroy your inner peace. - Dalai Lama

. . .

The mind is everything. What you think, you become. - Buddha

I just want you to know that if you are out there and you are being really hard on yourself right now for something that has happened ... it's normal. That is what is going to happen to you in life. No one gets through unscathed. We are all going to have a few scratches on us. Please be kind to yourselves and stand up for yourself, please. - Taylor Swift

Never be ashamed of yourself. Be proud of who you are and don't worry about how others see you. -Kristen Butler

I have learned that people will forget what you've said. People forget what you did. But people will never forget how you them feel. - Maya Angelou

The meaning of life is to find your gift. The purpose of life is to give it away. - Pablo Picasso

A bird does not sing because it has an answer. He sings because it has a song. - Joan Aknglund

Yu will never reach your destination, if you stop and throw stones at every dog that barks. - Winston Churchill

Don't be afraid to start again. This time, you're not starting from scratch, you're starting from experience. - Peter Hayden Dinklage

. . .

If you hate, then you have been defeated. - Confucius

Sometimes you find exactly what you're, where looking for before you even realized you were looking for it. Stay open. Stay positive. Things can change overnight. - Doe Zantamata

Forging people in silence and never talking to them again is a form of self-care. - Denzel Washington

I fear not the man who practiced 10000 kicks once, but I fear the man who has practice one kick 10000 times. - Bruce Lee

I am okay with being a 'Loner' and having a 'Small Circle'. I enjoy my own company and only want to be around people who genuinely enjoy me. - Keanu Reeves

The more chances you give someone, the less respect they'll start to have for you. They'll begin to ignore the standards that you've set because they'll know another chance will always be given. They're not afraid to lose you because they know no matter what you won't walk away. They get comfortable with depending on your forgiveness. Never let a person get comfortable disrespecting you. - Trent Shelton

Forgive anyone who has caused you pain or harm. Keep in mind that forgiving is not for others. It is for you. Forgiving is not forgetting. It frees up your power, heals your body, mind and spirit. Forgiveness opens up a pathway to a new place of peace where you can persist despite what has happened to you. - Les Brown

. . .

The way to gain a good reputation is to endeavor to what you desire to appear. - Socrates

Go out into the world with your passion and love for what you do, and just never give up. - Dianne Reeve

When people walk away from you, let them go. Your destiny is never tied to anyone who leaves you, and it doesn't mean they are bad people. It just means their part in your story is over. - T.D. Jakes

When you know what a man wants you know who he is and how to move him. - Petyr Baelish

Big results require big ambitions. - Heraclitus

Never forget what you are. The rest of the world will not. Wear it like armor, and it can never be used to hurt you. - Tyrion Lannister

A man with no motive is a man no one suspects. Always keep your foes confused. If they are never certain who you are or what you want, they cannon know what you are likely to do next. - Pentyl Baelish

Pay attention to your enemies, for they are the first to discover your mistakes. - Antisthenes

. . .

Success consists of going from failure to failure without loss of enthusiasm. - Winston Churchill

Failure is a part of life. If you don't fail, you don't learn. If you don't learn, you'll never change. - Morgan Freeman

When a person responds to the joys and sorrows of others as if they were his own, he has attained the highest state of spiritual union. - Bhagavad Gite

Don't force yourself to fit in where you don't belong. - Tiffany M. Hart

Never waste your time trying to explain yourself to people who are committed to misunderstanding you. - Lil Wayne Feat

The purpose of our lives is to be happy. - Dalai Lama

It's time to slow down and allow your body and mind rest. -Ludwig Van Beethov

The greatest weapon against stress is our ability to choose one thought over another. - William James.

It is better to have less thunder in the mouth and more lightning in the heart. - Native American Wisdom

. . .

Two things you will never have to chase: True friends & true love. - Mandy Hale

Being kind is very important. But most importantly, be kind to yourself. Because the true practice of love and kindness starts with self-love and self-kindness. - Ravindra Kumar A

Worry is a total waste of time. It doesn't change anything. All it does is steal your joy and keep you busy doing nothing. - Helen Barry

If you learn to really sit with loneliness and embrace it for the gift that it is...an opportunity to get to know YOU, to learn how strong you really are, to depend on no one but YOU for your happiness... you will realize that a little loneliness goes a LONG way in creating a richer, deeper, more vibrant and colorful you. - Mandy Hale

You are essentially who you create yourself to be and all that occurs in your life is the result of your own making. - Stephen Richards

Learn to be pleased with everything...because it could always be worse, but isn't! - Plutarch

If you have a dream, don't just sit there. Gather courage to believe that you can succeed and leave no stone unturned to make it a reality. - Roopleen

Minds are like flowers, they only open when the time is right. - Stephen Richards

. . .

Get going. Move forward. Aim High. Plan a takeoff. Don't just sit on the runway and hope someone will come along and push the airplane. It simply won't happen. Change your attitude and gain some altitude. Believe me, you'll love it up here. - Donald J. Trump

You'll learn, as you get older, that rules are made to be broken. Be bold enough to live life on your terms, and never, ever apologize for it. Go against the grain, refuse to conform, take the road less traveled instead of the well-beaten path. Laugh in the face of adversity, and leap before you look. Dance as though everybody is watching. March to the beat of your own drummer. And stubbornly refuse to fit in. - Mandy Hale

Sometimes it takes a heartbreak to shake us awake & help us see we are worth so much more than we're settling for. -Mandy Hale, The Single Woman: Life, Love, and a Dash of Sass. Think like a man of action, and act like a man of thought. - Henri L. Bergson

I am only one, but still, I am one. I cannot do everything, but still, I can do something. And because I cannot do everything, I will not refuse to do the something that I can do. - Hellen Keller

Half of the troubles of this life can be traced to saying yes too quickly and not saying no soon enough. - Josh Billings

Your time is limited, so don't waste it living someone else's life. Don't be trapped by dogma – which is living with the results of other people's thinking. - Steve Jobs

. . .

Not how long, but how well you have lived is the main thing. - Seneca

If life were predictable it would cease to be life, and be without flavor. - Eleanor Roosevelt

The whole secret of a successful life is to find out what is one's destiny to do, and then do it. - Henry Ford

In order to write about life first you must live it. - Ernest Hemingway

The big lesson in life, baby, is never be scared of anyone or anything. - Frank Sinatra

Even if you're on the right track, you'll get run over if you just sit there. - Will Rogers

Man, often becomes what he believes himself to be. If I keep on saying to myself that I cannot do a certain thing, it is possible that I may end by really becoming incapable of doing it. On the contrary, if I have the belief that I can do it, I shall surely acquire the capacity to do it even if I may not have it at the beginning. - Mahatma Gandhi

. . .

You can never cross the ocean unless you have the courage to lose sight of the shore. - Christopher Columbus

To a brave man, good and bad luck are like his left and right hand. He uses both. – St. Catherine of Siena

When one door of happiness closes, another opens, but often we took so long at the closed door that we do not see the one that has been opened up for us. - Helen Keller

We don't see the things the way they are. We see things the way we are. - Talmund

Every problem has in it the seeds of its own solution. If you don't have any problems, you don't get any seeds. - Norman Vincent Peale

If you change the way you look at things, the things you look at change. – Dr. Wayne Dyer

The problem is not that there are problems. The problem is expecting otherwise and thinking that having problems is a problem. - Theodore Rubin

Opportunity is missed by most people because it is dressed in overalls and looks like work. - Thomas A Edison

. . .

Blessed is those who can give without remembering and take without forgetting. - Elizabeth Bibesco

Yesterday is history, tomorrow is a mystery. And today? Today is a gift. That's why we call it the present. – B. Olatunji

When you get to the end of the rope, tie a knot and hang on. - Franklin D Roosevelt

Your attitude, not your aptitude, determines your altitude. – Zig Ziglar

If you're going through hell, keep going. – Winston Churchill

The secret to success is to start from scratch and keep on scratching. - Dennis Green

It is more shameful to distrust our friends than to be deceived by them. – Confucius

In all things, it is better to hope than despair. - Johann van Goethe

Champions aren't made in gyms. Champions are made from something they have deep inside them a desire, a dream, a vision. They have to have the skill and the will. But the will must be stronger than the skill. – Muhammad Ali

. . .

Most of the important things in the world have been accomplished by people who have kept on trying when there seemed to be no hope at all. - Dale Carnegie

So many of our dreams at first seems impossible, then they seem improbable, and then, when we summon the will, they soon become inevitable. - Christopher Reeve

Hard work spotlights the character of people. Some turn up their sleeves. Some turn up their noses, and some don't turn up at all. - Sam Ewing

Our greatest glory is not in never falling, but in rising every time we fall. - Confucious

There are those who work all day. Those who dream all day. And those who spend an hour dreaming before setting to work to fulfill those dreams. Go into the third category because there's virtually no competition. - Steven J Ross

It is your road and yours alone. Others may walk it with you, but no one can walk it for you. Accept yourself and your actions. Own your thoughts. Speak up when wrong, and apologize. Know your path at all times. To do this must know yourself inside and out, accept your gifts as well as your shortcomings, and grow each day with honesty, integrity, compassion, faith, and brotherhood. - Ursula Altenburg (Native and Cherokee Beauty)

. . .

Many of life's failures are people who had not realized how close they were to success when they gave up. – Thomas A Edison

The main thing is to keep the main thing the main thing. – Stephen Covey

Efficiency is doing things right. Effectiveness is doing the right things. – Peter Drucker

If life were predictable it would cease to be life and be without flavor. - Eleanor Roosevelt

In the end, it's not the years in your life that count. It's the life in your years. - Abraham Lincoln

Life is a succession of lessons which must be lived to be understood. - Ralph Waldo Emerson

You will face many defeats in life, but never let yourself be defeated. - Maya Angelou

Never let the fear of striking out keep you from playing the game. - Babe Ruth

Life is never fair, and perhaps it is a good thing for most of us that it is not. - Oscar Wilde

. . .

The only impossible journey is the one you never begin. -Tony Robbins

In this life we cannot do great things. We can only do small things with great love. - Mother Teresa

I will no longer allow the negative things in life to spoil all of the good things I have. I choose to be happy. - Helen Barry

No matter how cool, talented, educated, or rich you are, how you treat people tells everything about you. Always remember integrity is everything. - Ravindra Kumar A.

Only a life lived for others is a life worthwhile. - Albert Einstein

The purpose of our lives is to be happy. - Dalai Lama

Life is what happens when you're busy making other plans. - John Lennon

You only live once, but if you do it right, once is enough. - Mae West

Live in the sunshine, swim the sea, drink the wild air. -Ralph Waldo Emerson

. . .

Go confidently in the direction of your dreams! Live the life you've imagined. - Henry David Thoreau

The greatest glory in living lies not in never falling, but in rising every time we fall. - Nelson Mandela

Life is really simple, but we insist on making it complicated. - Confucius

May you live all the days of your life. - Jonathan Swift

Life itself is the most wonderful fairy tale. - Hans Christian Andersen

Do not let making a living prevent you from making a life. - John Wooden

Life is ours to be spent, not to be saved. - D. H. Lawrence

Do you know what happens when you give a procrastinator a good idea? Nothing. - Donald Gardner

Success is what you attract by the person you become. – Jim Rohn

You have to 'Be' before you can 'Do' and 'Do' before you can 'Have.'- Zig Ziglar

. . .

Some people think that to be strong is to never feel the pain. In reality the strongest people are the ones who feel it, understand it, and accept it. - Helen Barry

You can have everything in life that you want if you will just help enough other people to get what they want. – Zig Ziglar

The test we must set for ourselves is not to march alone but to march in such a way that others wish to join us. – Hubert Humphrey

Lots of people want to ride with you in the limo, but what you want is someone who will take the bus when the limo breaks down. - Oprah Winfrey

The deepest pain I ever felt was denying my own feelings to make everyone else comfortable. – Nicole Lyons

When people say they can't see anything good in you, hug them and say life is difficult for the blind. – Leonardo DiCaprio

Give the ones you love wings to fly, roots to come back, and reasons to stay. – Dalai Lama

Formal education will make you a living. Self-education will make you a fortune. - Jim Rohn

. . .

Live your beliefs and you can turn the world around. – Henry David Thoreau

We must let go of the life we have planned, so as to accept the one that is waiting for us. – Josep Cambell

Find out who you are and be that person. That's what your soul was put on this earth to be. Find hat truth live that truth, and everything else will be come. - Ellen DeGeneres

Real change, enduring change, happens one step at a time. – Ruth Bader Ginsburg

Your gain strength, courage, and confidence by every experience in which you really stop to look fear in the face. You are able to say to yourself, 'I lived through this horror. I can take the next thing that comes along'. You must do the thing you cannot do. – Eleanor Roosevelt.

Our lives are stories in which we write, direct and star in the leading role. Some chapters are happy, while others being lessons to learn, but we always have the power to be the heroes of our adventures. – Joelle Speranza

Life is like riding a bicycle. To keep your balance, you must keep moving. – Albert Eistein

. . .

It isn't what the book costs. It's what it will cost you if you don't read it. - Jim Rohn

You must be the change you want to see in the world. – Mahatma Gandhi

The future has several names. For the weak, it is the impossible. For the fainthearted, it is the unknown. For the thoughtful and valiant, it is the ideal. – Victor Hugo

There is nothing more genuine than breaking away from the chorus to learn the sound of your own voice. – Po Bronson

Do not go where the path may lead, go instead where there is no path and leave a trail. – Waldo Emerson

Use what talents you possess; the woods will be very silent if no birds sang there except those that sang best. – Henry van Dyke

Do not fear to be eccentric in opinion, for every opinion now accepted was once eccentric. – Bertrand Russell

History will be kind to me, for I intend to write it. – Winston Churchill

Life isn't about finding yourself. Life's about creating yourself. – George Bernard Shaw

. . .

Live your life each day as you would climb a mountain. An occasional glance towards the summit keeps the goal in mind, but many beautiful scenes are to be observed from each new vintage point. – Harold B Melchart

The tragedy of life doesn't lie in not reaching your goal. The tragedy lies in having no goals to reach. – Benjamin Mays

An excuse is worse and more terrible than a lie, for an excuse is a lie guarded. – Pope John Paul I

Don't wish it were easier, wish you were better. Don't wish for fewer problems, wish for more skills. Don't wish for less challenges, wish for more wisdom. – Earl Shoaf

Yesterday is not ours to recover, but tomorrow is ours to win or lose. - Lyndon B. Johnson

Imagine your life is perfect in every respect; what would it look like? - Brian Tracy

The stupid neither forgive or forget. The naïve forgive and forget. The wise forgive, but do not forget. – Thomas Szasz

Challenges are what make life interesting. Overcoming them is what makes them meaningful. – Joshua Marine

. . .

The future belongs to the competent. Get good, get better, be the best. - Brian Tracy

When you have a dream, you've got to grab it and never let go. - Carol Burnett

Nothing is impossible. The word itself says 'I'm possible! - Audrey Hepburn

There is nothing impossible to they who will try. - Alexander the Great

The bad news is time flies. The good news is you're the pilot. - Michael Altshuler

Get busy living or get busy dying. - Stephen King

You only live once, but if you do it right, once is enough. - Mae West

Many of life's failures are people who did not realize how close they were to success when they gave up. - Thomas A. Edison

If you want to live a happy life, tie it to a goal, not to people or things. - Albert Einstein

. . .

Never let the fear of striking out keep you from playing the game. - Babe Ruth

Money and success don't change people; they merely amplify what is already there. - Willy Smith

If life were predictable it would cease to be life, and be without flavor. - Eleanor Roosevelt

Your time is limited, so don't waste it living someone else's life. Don't be trapped by dogma – which is living with the results of other people's thinking. - Steve Jobs

Not how long, but how well you have lived is the main thing. - Seneca

The whole secret of a successful life is to find out what is one's destiny to do, and then do it. - Henry Ford

In order to write about life first you must live it. - Ernest Hemingway

The big lesson in life, baby, is never be scared of anyone or anything. - Frank Sinatra

. . .

Curiosity about life in all of its aspects, I think, is still the secret of great creative people. – Leo Burnett

The unexamined life is not worth living. - Socrates

Be happy with what you have, while working for what you want. - Helen Barry

Life is not a problem to be solved, but a reality to be experienced. – Soren Kierkegaard

Turn your wounds into wisdom. - Oprah Winfrey

The way I see it, if you want the rainbow, you got to put up with the rain. - Dolly Parton

Don't settle for what life gives you; make life better and build something. - Ashton Kutcher

Everybody wants to be famous, but nobody wants to do the work. I live by that. You grind hard so you can play hard. At the end of the day, you put all the work in, and eventually it'll pay off. It could be in a year; it could be in 30 years. Eventually, your hard work will pay off. - Kevin Hart

Everything negative – pressure, challenges – is all an opportunity for me to rise. - Kobe Bryant

. . .

I like criticism. It makes you strong. - LeBron James

You never really learn much from hearing yourself speak. - George Clooney

Life imposes things on you that you can't control, but you still have the choice of how you're going to live through this. - Celine Dion

Life is never easy. There is work to be done and obligations to be met obligations to truth, to justice, and to liberty. - John F. Kennedy

Live for each second without hesitation. - Elton John

Life is like riding a bicycle. To keep your balance, you must keep moving. - Albert Einstein

Life is really simple, but men insist on making it complicated. - Confucius

Life is a succession of lessons which must be lived to be understood. - Helen Keller

Your work is going to fill a large part of your life, and the only way to be truly satisfied is to do what you believe is great work. And the only way to do great work is to love what you do. If you haven't found it yet, keep looking. Don't settle. As with all matters of the heart, you'll know when you find it. - Steve Jobs

My mama always said, life is like a box of chocolates. You never know what you're going to get. - Forrest Gump

Watch your thoughts; they become words. Watch your words; they become actions. Watch your actions; they become habits. Watch your habits; they become character. Watch your character; it becomes your destiny. - Lao-Tze

To fail to do good is as bad as doing harm. - Plutarch

When we do the best, we can, we never know what miracle is wrought in our life or the life of another. - Helen Keller

The healthiest response to life is joy. - Deepak Chopra

Life is like a coin. You can spend it any way you wish, but you only spend it once. - Lillian Dickson

The best portion of a good man's life is his little nameless, unencumbered acts of kindness and of love. - Wordsworth

s I can sum up everything I've learned about life: It
ert Frost

. . .

Life is ten percent what happens to you and ninety percent how you respond to it. - Charles Swindoll

Keep calm and carry on. - Winston Churchill

Maybe that's what life is a wink of the eye and winking stars. - Jack Kerouac

Life is a flower of which love is the honey. - Victor Hugo

Keep smiling, because life is a beautiful thing and there's so much to smile about. - Marilyn Monroe

Health is the greatest gift, contentment the greatest wealth, faithfulness the best relationship. - Buddha

You have brains in your head. You have feet in your shoes. You can steer yourself any direction you choose. - Dr. Seuss

Good friends, good books, and a sleepy conscience: this is the ideal life. - Mark Twain

Something having coffee with your best friend, is all of the therapy you need. - Helen Barry

Life would be tragic if it weren't funny. - Stephen Hawking

. . .

Live in the sunshine, swim the sea, drink the wild air. - Ralph Waldo Emerson

The greatest pleasure of life is love. - Euripides

Life is what we make it, always has been, always will be. - Grandma Moses

Life's tragedy is that we get old too soon and wise too late. - Benjamin Franklin

Life is about making an impact, not making an income. - Kevin Kruse

I've missed more than 9000 shots in my career. I've lost almost 300 games. 26 times I've been trusted to take the game winning shot and missed. I've failed over and over and over again in my life. And that is why I succeed. - Michael Jordan

Every strike brings me closer to the next home run. - Babe Ruth

The two most important days in your life are the day you are born and the day you find out why. - Mark Twain

Life shrinks or expands in proportion to one's courage. - Anais Nin

. . .

When I was 5 years old, my mother always told me that happiness was the key to life. When I went to school, they asked me what I wanted to be when I grew up. I wrote down 'happy'. They told me I didn't understand the assignment, and I told them they didn't understand life. - John Lennon

Too many of us are not living our dreams because we are living our fears. - Les Brown

I believe every human has a finite number of heartbeats. I don't intend to waste any of mine. - Neil Armstrong

Live as if you were to die tomorrow. Learn as if you were to live forever. - Mahatma Gandhi

If you live long enough, you'll make mistakes. But if you learn from them, you'll be a better person. - Bill Clinton

Life is short, and it is here to be lived. - Kate Winslet

The longer I live, the more beautiful life becomes. - Frank Lloyd Wright

Every moment is a fresh beginning. -T.S. Eliot

. . .

When you cease to dream you cease to live. - Malcolm Forbes

If you spend your whole life waiting for the storm, you'll never enjoy the sunshine. - Morris West

Don't cry because it's over, smile because it happened. -Dr. Seuss

If you can do what you do best and be happy, you're further along in life than most people. - Leonardo DiCaprio

We should remember that just as a positive outlook on life can promote good health, so can everyday acts of kindness. - Hillary Clinton

Don't limit yourself. Many people limit themselves to what they think they can do. You can go as far as your mind lets you. What you believe, remember, you can achieve. - Mary Kay Ash

It is our choices that show what we truly are, far more than our abilities. - J. K. Rowling

If you're not stubborn, you'll give up on experiments too soon. And if you're not flexible, you'll pound your head against the wall and you won't see a different solution to a problem you're trying to solve. - Jeff Bezos

. . .

The best way to predict your future is to create it. - Abraham Lincoln

You must expect great things of yourself before you can do them. - Michael Jordan

There are no mistakes, only opportunities. -Tina Fey

Identity is a prison you can never escape, but the way to redeem your past is not to run from it, but to try to understand it, and use it as a foundation to grow. - Jay-Z

As you grow older, you will discover that you have two hands, one for helping yourself, the other for helping others. - Audrey Hepburn

Sometimes you can't see yourself clearly until you see yourself through the eyes of others. - Ellen DeGeneres

You must not lose faith in humanity. Humanity is an ocean; if a few drops of the ocean are dirty, the ocean does not become dirty. - Mahatma Gandhi

All life is an experiment. The more experiments you make, the better. - Ralph Waldo Emerson

. . .

It had long since come to my attention that people of accomplishment rarely sat back and let things happen to them. They went out and happened to things. - Leonardo Da Vinci

Throughout life people will make you mad, disrespect you and treat you bad. Let God deal with the things they do, cause hate in your heart will consume you too. - Will Smith

Don't try to lessen yourself for the world; let the world catch up to you. – Beyonce

When it comes to luck, you make your own. – Bruce Springsteen

If you don't like the road you're walking, start paving another ore. – Dolly Parton

I have learned over the years that one's mind is made up, this diminishes fear; knowing what must be done away always with fear. – Rosa Parks

The moral of my story is the sun always comes out after the storm. Being optimistic and surrounding yourself wit positive loving people is for me, living life in the sunny side of the street. – Janice Dean

We generate fears while we sit. We overcome them by action. – Dr. Henry Link

. . .

We are not our best intentions. We are what we do. – Amy Dickinson

Here's to the crazy ones, the misfits, the rebels, the troublemakers, the round pegs in the square holes, the ones who see things differently they're not fond of rules. You can quote them, disagree with them, glorify or vilify them, but the only thing you can't do is ignore them because they change things. They push the human race forward, and while some may see them as the crazy ones, we see genius. - Steve Jobs

Do not dwell in the past, do not dream of the future, concentrate the mind on the present moment. - Buddha

Life is a dream for the wise, a game for the fool, a comedy for the rich, a tragedy for the poor. - Sholom Aleichem

If you love life, don't waste time, for time is what life is made up of. - Bruce Lee

When one door closes, another opens; but we often look so long and so regretfully upon the closed door that we do not see the one that has opened for us. – Alexander Graham Bell

Be happy for this moment. This moment is your life. - Omar Khayyam

. . .

Happiness is the feeling that power increases that resistance is being overcome. - Friedrich Nietzsche

I have learned to seek my happiness by limiting my desires, rather than in attempting to satisfy them. - John Stuart Mill

The secret of happiness, you see is not found in seeking more, but in developing the capacity to enjoy less. -Socrates

The more man meditates upon good thoughts; the better will be his world and the world at large. - Confucius

The greatest blessings of mankind are within us and within our reach. A wise man is content with his lot, whatever it may be, without wishing for what he has not. - Seneca

Happiness is like a butterfly; the more you chase it, the more it will elude you, but if you turn your attention to other things, it will come and sit softly on your shoulder. - Henry David Thoreau

When it is obvious that goals can't be reached, don't adjust the goals, but adjust the action steps. - Confucius

There may be people who have more talent than you, but there's no excuse for anyone to work harder than you do – and I believe that. - Derek Jeter

. . .

Don't be afraid to fail. It's not the end of the world, and in many ways, it's the first step toward learning something and getting better at it. - Jon Hamm

Life is very interesting... in the end, some of your greatest pains, become your greatest strengths. - Drew Barrymore

I think if you live in a black-and-white world, you're going to suffer a lot. I used to be like that. But I don't believe that anymore. - Bradley Cooper

Don't allow silly drama to stress you out. Breathe and let it go. - Helen Barry

I don't believe in happy endings, but I do believe in happy travels, because ultimately, you die at a very young age, or you live long enough to watch your friends die. It's a mean thing, life. - George Clooney

It's never too late – never too late to start over, never too late to be happy. - Jane Fonda

You're only human. You live once and life is wonderful, so eat the damned red velvet cupcake. - Emma Stone

A lot of people give up just before they're about to make it. You know you never know when that next obstacle is going to be the last one. - Chuck Norris

. . .

Be nice to people on the way up, because you may meet them on the way down. - Jimmy Durante

I believe you make your day. You make your life. So much of it is all perception, and this is the form that I built for myself. I have to accept it and work within those compounds, and it's up to me. - Brad Pitt

The minute that you're not learning I believe you're dead. - Jack Nicholson

Life's tough, but it's tougher when you're stupid. - John Wayne

I guess it comes down to a simple choice, really. Get busy living or get busy dying. - Shawshank Redemption

When we strive to become better than we are, everything around us becomes better too. - Paulo Coelho

In the long run, the sharpest weapon of all is a kind and gentle spirit. - Anne Frank

You only pass through this life once; you don't come back for an encore. - Elvis Presley

. . .

Happy is the man who can make a living by his hobby. - George Bernard Shaw

Be where you are; otherwise, you will miss your life. - Buddha

Living an experience, a particular fate, is accepting it fully. - Albert Camus

The more you praise and celebrate your life, the more there is in life to celebrate. - Oprah Winfrey

Your image isn't your character. Character is what you are as a person. - Derek Jeter

Football is like life, it requires perseverance, self-denial, hard work sacrifice, dedication and respect for authority. - Vince Lombardi

As you know, life is an echo; we get what we give. - David DeNotaris

There are no regrets in life, just lessons. - Jennifer Aniston

Believe that nothing in life is unimportant every moment can be a beginning. - John McLeod

Find people who will make you better. - Michelle Obama

. . .

As my knowledge of things grew, I felt more and more the delight of the world I was in. - Helen Keller

Benjamin Franklin was a humanitarian that dedicated his life to making contributions to all humans. He had a clear purpose for himself: improve the human race. - Paulo Braga

My mission in life is not merely to survive, but to thrive; and to do so with some passion, some compassion, some humor, and some style. - Maya Angelou

If we don't change, we don't grow. If we don't grow, we aren't really living. - Gail Sheehy

You choose the life you live. If you don't like it, it's on you to change it because no one else is going to do it for you. - Kim Kiyosaki

Life doesn't require that we be the best, only that we try our best. H. Jackson Brown Jr.

Life isn't about waiting for the storm to pass; it's about learning to dance in the rain. - Vivian Greene

I enjoy life when things are happening. I don't care if it's good things or bad things. That means you're alive. - Joan Rivers

. . .

Make each day your masterpiece. - John Wooden

The way I see it, every life is a pile of good things and bad things. The good things don't always soften the bad things, but vice versa, the bad things don't always spoil the good things and make them unimportant. - Doctor Who

There's more to life than basketball. The most important thing is your family and taking care of each other and loving each other no matter what." – Stephen Curry

Today, you have 100% of your life left. - Tom Landry

Nobody who ever gave his best regretted it. - George Halas

You can't put a limit on anything. The more you dream, the farther you get. - Michael Phelps

Life is about making an impact, not making an income. - Kevin Kruse

Whatever the mind of man can conceive and believe, it can achieve. – Napoleon Hill

Strive not to be a success, but rather to be of value. – Albert Einstein

. . .

Two roads diverged in a wood, and I took the one less traveled by, and that has made all the difference. – Robert Frost

I attribute my success to this: I never gave or took any excuse. – Florence Nightingale

You miss 100% of the shots you don't take. – Wayne Gretzky

I've missed more than 9000 shots in my career. I've lost almost 300 games. 26 times I've been trusted to take the game winning shot and missed. I've failed over and over and over again in my life. And that is why I succeed. – Michael Jordan

Time is the wisest of all counselors. - Plutarch

The most difficult thing is the decision to act, the rest is merely tenacity. – Amelia Earhart

Every strike brings me closer to the next home run. – Babe Ruth

Definiteness of purpose is the starting point of all achievement. - W. Clement Stone

Life isn't about getting and having, it's about giving and being. – Kevin Kruse

. . .

Don't be impressed by money, followers, degrees and titles. Be impressed by kindness, integrity, humility and generosity. - Helen Barry

Life is what happens to you while you're busy making other plans. - John Lennon

We become what we think about. - Earl Nightingale

The cure for pain is in the pain. - Rumi

Twenty years from now you will be more disappointed by the things that you didn't do than by the ones you did do, so throw off the bowlines, sail away from safe harbor, catch the trade winds in your sails. Explore, Dream, Discover. - Mark Twain

Life is 10% what happens to me and 90% of how I react to it. - Charles Swindoll

The most common way people give up their power is by thinking they don't have any. - Alice Walker

The mind is everything. What you think you become. - Buddha

An unexamined life is not worth living. - Socrates

. . .

Eighty percent of success is showing up. – Woody Allen

Your time is limited, so don't waste it living someone else's life. – Steve Jobs

Winning isn't everything, but wanting to win is. – Vince Lombardi

I am not a product of my circumstances. I am a product of my decisions. – Stephen Covey

Every child is an artist. The problem is how to remain an artist once he grows up. – Pablo Picasso

The most painful tears are not the ones that fall from your eyes and cover your face. They're the ones that fall from your heart and cover your soul. - Amy Liferhino

Never give in never, never, never, in nothing great or small, large or petty, never give in except to convictions of honor and good sense. Never yield to force; never yield or the apparently overwhelming might of the enemy. - Winston Churchill

Don't let anyone break you. There may always be people who secretly want to see you fail. That's okay. Just stay strong and stand tall. - Kristen Butler

. . .

If you want to be happy, set a goal that commands your thoughts, liberates your energy and inspires your hopes. - Andrew Carnegie

Success is the progressive realization of a worthy goal or ideal. - Earl Nightingale

The trouble with not having a goal is that you can spend your life running up and down the field and never score. - Bill Copeland

I think goals should never be easy, they should force you to work, even if they are uncomfortable at the time. - Michael Phelps

You can never cross the ocean until you have the courage to lose sight of the shore. – Christopher Columbus

Sometimes we forgive not because we are wrong, but because staying angry robs us of happiness. - Helen Barry

Either you run the day, or the day runs you. – Jim Rohn

I've learned that people will forget what you said, people will forget what you did, but people will never forget how you made them feel. – Maya Angelou

A few vices are sufficient to darken many virtues. - Plutarch

. . .

Whether you think you can or you think you can't, you're right. – Henry Ford

The two most important days in your life are the day you are born and the day you find out why. – Mark Twain

Whatever you can do, or dream you can, begin it. Boldness has genius, power and magic in it. – Johann Wolfgang von Goethe

The best revenge is massive success. –Frank Sinatra

People often say that motivation doesn't last. Well, neither does bathing. That's why we recommend it daily. – Zig Ziglar

Life shrinks or expands in proportion to one's courage. – Anais Nin

Life with you is all the meanings of happiness. - Dr. Abeer

If you hear a voice within you say "you cannot paint," then by all means paint and that voice will be silenced. – Vincent Van Gogh

There is only one way to avoid criticism: do nothing, say nothing, and be nothing. – Aristotle

The only person you are destined to become is the person you decide to be. – Ralph Waldo Emerson

. . .

Go confidently in the direction of your dreams. Live the life you have imagined. – Henry David Thoreau

The older I get, the more I understand that it's okay to live life others don't understand. Dr. Abeer

The most beautiful eyes are those that seek beauty in others. - Dr. Abeer

So many books, so little time. - Frank Zappa

Darkness cannot drive out darkness: only light can do that. Hate cannot drive out hate: only love can do that. - Martin Luther King Jr.

We suffer more in our imagination than in reality. – Seneca

It's never too late to be what you might have been. - George Elliot

Our life is what is what our thoughts make it. - Marcus Aurelius

Thinking is difficult, that's why most people judge. - Cario

. . .

When I stand before God at the end of my life, I would hope that I would not have a single bit of talent left and could say, I used everything you gave me. – Erma Bombeck

Few things can help an individual more than to place responsibility on him, and to let him know that you trust him. – Booker T. Washington

Certain things catch your eye, but pursue only those that capture the heart. – Ancient Indian Proverb

Believe you can and you're halfway there. –Theodore Roosevelt

The way you see people is the way you treat them, and the way you treat them is what they become. – Johann Wolfgang von Goethe

Everything you've ever wanted is on the other side of fear. – George Addair

We can easily forgive a child who is afraid of the dark; the real tragedy of life is when men are afraid of the light. – Plato

Teach thy tongue to say, "I do not know," and thus shalt progress. – Maimonides

Start where you are. Use what you have. Do what you can. – Arthur Ashe

. . .

How wonderful it is that nobody need wait a single moment before starting to improve the world. – Anne Frank

When I was 5 years old, my mother always told me that happiness was the key to life. When I went to school, they asked me what I wanted to be when I grew up. I wrote down 'happy'. They told me I didn't understand the assignment, and I told them they didn't understand life. – John Lennon

When one door of happiness closes, another opens, but often we look so long at the closed door that we do not see the one that has been opened for us. – Helen Keller

Everything has beauty, but not everyone can see. – Confucius

When I let go of what I am, I become what I might be. – Lao Tzu

Life is not measured by the number of breaths we take, but by the moments that take our breath away. – Maya Angelou

Happiness is not something readymade. It comes from your own actions. – Dalai Lama

If you're offered a seat on a rocket ship, don't ask what seat! Just get on. – Sheryl Sandberg

. . .

Magic is believing in yourself, if you can d hat, you can make anything happen. – Johann Wolfgang von Goethe

We must believe that we are gifted for something, and that this thing, at whatever cost, must be attained. – Marie Curie

Too many of us are not living our dreams because we are living our fears. – Les Brown

Challenges are what make life interesting and overcoming them is what makes life meaningful. – Joshua J. Marine

If you want to lift yourself up, lift up someone else. – Booker T. Washington

I have been impressed with the urgency of doing. Knowing is not enough; we must apply. Being willing is not enough; we must do. – Leonardo da Vinci

Limitations live only in our minds. But if we use our imaginations, our possibilities become limitless. – Jamie Paolinetti

You take your life in your own hands, and what happens? A terrible thing, no one to blame. – Erica Jong

What's money? A man is a success if he gets up in the morning and goes to bed at night and in between does what he wants to do. – Bob Dylan

I didn't fail the test. I just found 100 ways to do it wrong. – Benjamin Franklin

In order to succeed, your desire for success should be greater than your fear of failure. – Bill Cosby

A person who never made a mistake never tried anything new. – Albert Einstein

The soul that sees beauty may sometimes walk alone. – Johann Wolfgang von Goethe

There are no traffic jams along the extra mile. – Roger Staubach

It is never too late to be what you might have been. – George Eliot

You become what you believe. – Oprah Winfrey

I would rather die of passion than of boredom. –Vincent van Gogh

It is not what you do for your children, but what you have taught them to do for themselves, that will make them successful human beings. – Ann Landers

. . .

If you want your children to turn out well, spend twice as much time with them, and half as much money. – Abigail Van Buren

Build your own dreams, or someone else will hire you to build theirs. – Farrah Gray

The battles that count aren't the ones for gold medals. The struggles within yourself--the invisible battles inside all of us--that's where it's at. – Jesse Owens

Education costs money. But then so does ignorance. – Sir Claus Moser

I have learned over the years that when one's mind is made up, this diminishes fear. – Rosa Parks

It does not matter how slowly you go as long as you do not stop. – Confucius

If you look at what you have in life, you'll always have more. If you look at what you don't have in life, you'll never have enough. – Oprah Winfrey

Remember that not getting what you want is sometimes a wonderful stroke of luck. – Dalai Lama

. . .

You can't use up creativity. The more you use, the more you have. – Maya Angelou

Behavior is the mirror in which everyone shows their image. – Johann Wolfgang von Goethe

Dream big and dare to fail. – Norman Vaughan

Our lives begin to end the day we become silent about things that matter. – Martin Luther King Jr.

Do what you can, where you are, with what you have. – Teddy Roosevelt

If you do what you've always done, you'll get what you've always gotten. - Tony Robbins

Dreaming, after all, is a form of planning. – Gloria Steinem

It's your place in the world; it's your life. Go on and do all you can with it, and make it the life you want to live. – Mae Jemison

You may be disappointed if you fail, but you are doomed if you don't try. – Beverly Sills

. . .

Remember no one can make you feel inferior without your consent. – Eleanor Roosevelt

Life is what we make it, always has been, always will be. - Grandma Moses

The question isn't who is going to let me; it's who is going to stop me. - Ayn Rand

When everything seems to be going against you, remember that the airplane takes off against the wind, not with it. – Henry Ford

It's not the years in your life that count. It's the life in your years. - Abraham Lincoln

Change your thoughts and you change your world. – Norman Vincent Peale

Either write something worth reading or do something worth writing. – Benjamin Franklin

Nothing is impossible, the word itself says, "I'm possible!" – Audrey Hepburn

The only way to do great work is to love what you do. – Steve Jobs

. . .

If you can dream it, you can achieve it. – Zig Ziglar

We become what we think about. - Earl Nightingale.

People who are crazy enough to think they can change the world, are the ones who do. - Rob Siltanen

Optimism is the one quality more associated with success and happiness than any other. - Brian Tracy

Happiness is not something readymade. It comes from your own actions. - Dalai Lama

Correction does much, but encouragement do more. – Johann Wolfgang von Goethe

All our dreams can come true if we have the courage to pursue them. - Walt Disney

Success is not fatal; failure is not fatal: it is the courage to continue that counts. - Winston Churchill

When it comes to inspirational, encouraging quotes by successful people. - Winston Churchill

Believe you can and you're halfway there. - Theodore Roosevelt

. . .

I can't change the direction of the wind, but I can adjust my sails to always reach my destination. – Jimmy Dean

Move out of your comfort zone. You can only grow if you are willing to feel awkward and uncomfortable when you try something new. - Brian Tracy

It is our attitude at the beginning of a difficult task which, more than anything else, will affect its successful outcome. – William James

You are never too old to set another goal or to dream a new dream. - C.S. Lewis

We must be willing to let go of the life we planned so as to have the life that is waiting for us. – Joseph Campbell

Everything you've ever wanted is on the other side of fear. - George Addair

I can't change the direction of the wind, but I can adjust my sails to always reach my destination. – Jimmy Dean

None are more hopelessly enslaved than those who falsely believe they are free. – Johann Wolfgang von Goethe

. . .

Move out of your comfort zone. You can only grow if you are willing to feel awkward and uncomfortable when you try something new. - Brian Tracy

It is our attitude at the beginning of a difficult task which, more than anything else, will affect its successful outcome. - William James

You are never too old to set another goal or to dream a new dream. – C.S. Lewis

We must be willing to let go of the life we planned so as to have the life that is waiting for us. – Joseph Campbell

Everything you've ever wanted is on the other side of fear. - George Addair

You get what you give. – Jennifer Lopez

Your life only gets better when you get better. - Brian Tracy

Happiness is not by chance, but by choice. – Jim Rohn

Be the change that you wish to see in the world. - Mahatma Ghandi

. . .

If I cannot do great things, I can do small things in a great way. – Martin Luther King Jr.

We generate fears while we sit. We overcome them by action. – Dr. Henry Link

Today's accomplishments were yesterday's impossibilities. – Robert H. Schuller

Light tomorrow with today! – Elizabeth Barrett Browning

The only limit to our realization of tomorrow will be our doubts of today. – Franklin D. Roosevelt

Keep your face always toward the sunshine, and shadows will fall behind you. – Walt Whitman

The bad news is time flies. The good news is you're the pilot. – Michael Altshuler

Never limit yourself because of others' limited imagination; never limit others because of your own limited imagination. – Mae Jemison

Let us make our future now, and let us make our dreams tomorrow's reality. – Malala Yousafzai

. . .

Don't Let Yesterday Take Up Too Much of Today. – Will Rogers

For every reason it's not possible, there are hundreds of people who have faced the same circumstances and succeeded. – Jack Canfield

We may encounter many defeats but we must not be defeated. – Maya Angelou

You only live once, but if you do it right, once is enough. - Mae West

In three words I can sum up everything I've learned about life: it goes on. - Robert Frost

Life is what happens to us while we are making other plans. -Allen Saunders

I may not have gone where I intended to go, but I think I have ended up where I needed to be. - Douglas Adams

Life isn't about finding yourself. Life is about creating yourself. - George Bernard Shaw

Life is like riding a bicycle. To keep your balance, you must keep moving. - Albert Einstein

. . .

Nothing in life is to be feared, it is only to be understood. Now is the time to understand more, so that we may fear less. - Marie Curie

You are the sum total of everything you've ever seen, heard, eaten, smelled, been told, forgot - it's all there. Everything influences each of us, and because of that I try to make sure that my experiences are positive. - Maya Angelou

The best way to get started is to quit talking and begin doing. - Walt Disney

Leaders never use the word failure. They look upon setbacks as learning experiences. – Brian Tracy

There are no limits to what you can accomplish, except the limits you place on your own thinking. – Brian Tracy

Someone is sitting in the shade today because someone planted a tree a long time ago. – Warren Buffet

The pessimist sees difficulty in every opportunity. The optimist sees opportunity in every difficulty. – Winston Churchill

If you are working on something that you really care about, you don't have to be pushed. The vision pulls you. – Steve Jobs

. . .

Entrepreneurs are great at dealing with uncertainty and also very good at minimizing risk. That's the classic entrepreneur. – Mohnish Pabrai

What you lack in talent can be made up with desire, hustle and giving 110% all the time. – Don Zimmer

Every strike brings me closer to the next home run. - Babe Ruth

The two most important days in your life are the day you are born and the day you find out why. - Mark Twain

Life shrinks or expands in proportion to one's courage. - Anais Nin

When I was 5 years old, my mother always told me that happiness was the key to life. When I went to school, they asked me what I wanted to be when I grew up. I wrote down 'happy'. They told me I didn't understand the assignment, and I told them they didn't understand life. - John Lennon

Too many of us are not living our dreams because we are living our fears. - Les Brown

I believe every human has a finite number of heartbeats. I don't intend to waste any of mine. - Neil Armstrong

. . .

Live as if you were to die tomorrow. Learn as if you were to live forever. - Mahatma Gandhi

If you live long enough, you'll make mistakes. But if you learn from them, you'll be a better person. - Bill Clinton

Life is short, and it is here to be lived. - Kate Winslet

Security is mostly a superstition. Life is either a daring adventure or nothing. - Helen Keller

Creativity is intelligence having fun. – Albert Einstein

Knowing is not enough; we must apply. Wishing is not enough; we must do. – Johann Wolfgang Von Goethe

Develop an 'attitude of gratitude.' Say thank you to everyone you meet for everything you do. – Brian Tracy

To see what is right and not do is a lack of courage. – Confucius

A room without books is like a body without a soul. – Marcus Tullius Cicero

You've got to get up every morning with determination if you're going to go to bed with satisfaction. - George Lorimer F

. . .

Go as far as you can see; when you get there, you'll be able to see further. - Thomas Carlyle

Fake it until you make it! Act as if you had all the confidence, you require until it becomes your reality. – Brian Tracy

The worship most acceptable to God comes from a thankful and cheerful heart. - Plutarch

I think goals should never be easy, they should force you to work, even if they are uncomfortable at the time. – Michael Phelps

The only way to do great work is to love what you do. If you haven't found it yet, keep looking. Don't settle. – Steve Jobs

Leaders think and talk about the solutions. Followers think and talk about the problems. – Brian Tracy

Whether you think you can or think you can't, you're right. – Henry Ford

Integrity is the most valuable and respected quality of leadership. Always keep your word. – Brian Tracy

. . .

Dreams don't have to just be dreams. You can make it reality. If you just keep pushing and keep trying then eventually, you'll reach yourself. And if that takes a few years, ten that's great, but if it takes 10 or 20s, then that's part of the process. – Naomi Osaka

We've been making our own opportunities, and as you prove your worth and value to people, they can't put you in a box. You hustle it into happening, right? - Jennifer Lopez

What you get by achieving your goals is not as important as what you become by achieving your goals. – Zig Ziglar

Leaders set high standards. Refuse to tolerate mediocrity or poor performance. – Brian Tracy

I'm realizing how much I've diminishing my own power. I'm not doing that no more. – Alicia Kays

You are never too old to set another goal or to dream a new dream. – C. S. Lewis

I believe that if you'll just stand up and go, life will open up for you! Something just motivates you to keep moving. – Tine Turner

The simple act of listening to someone and making them feel as if they have truly been heard is most treasured gift. – L.A. Villafane

. . .

You have to be where you are to get where you need to go. – Amy Poehler

It is never too late to be what you might have been. – George Eliot

The only limit to our realization of tomorrow will be our doubts of today. – Franklin Deleno Roosevelt

We all have problems. Buy it's not what happens to us, it's the choices we make after. - Elizabeth Smart

The key responsibility of leadership is to think about the future. No one else can do it for you. – Brian Tracy

To conduct great matters and never commit a fault is above the force of human nature. - Plutarch

Your talent determines what you can do. Your motivation determines how much you're willing to do. Your attitude determines how well you do it. - Lou Holtz

It's not whether you get knocked down, it's whether you get back up. –Vince Lombardi

Failure will never overtake me if my determination to succeed is strong enough. – Og Mandino

. . .

Do what you can with all you have, wherever you are. – Theodore Roosevelt

One of the lessons that I grew up with was to always stay true to yourself and never let what somebody else says distract you from your goals. – Michelle Obama

You don't have to be great to start, but you have to start to be great. – Zig Ziglar

Folks are usually about as happy as they make up their minds to be. - Abraham Lincoln

If you don't like the road you're walking, start paving another one. – Dolly Parton

The happiness of your life depends on the quality of your thoughts. – Marcus Aurelius

Things work out best for those who make the best of how things work out. – John Wooden

My mission in life is not merely to survive, but to thrive. – Maya Angelou

. . .

Make your life a masterpiece, imagine no limitations on what you can be, have, or do. – Brian Tracy

Life changes very quickly, in a very positive way, if you let it. – Lindsey Vonn

Inspiration comes from within yourself. One has to be positive. When you're positive, good things happen. – Deep Roy

Change the world by being yourself. – Amy Poehler

Every moment is a fresh beginning. – T.S Eliot

Never regret anything that made you smile. – Mark Twain

There is no substitute for hard work. – Thomas Edison

May your choices reflect your hopes, not your fears. – Nelson Mandela

Turn your wounds into wisdom. – Oprah Winfrey

Change the game, don't let the game change you. - Macklemore

It hurt because it mattered. - John Green

. . .

Life has got all those twists and turns. You've got to hold on tight and off you go. - Nicole Kidman

Keep your face always toward the sunshine, and shadows will fall behind you. - Walt Whitman

Be courageous. Challenge orthodoxy. Stand up for what you believe in. When you are in your rocking chair talking to your grandchildren many years from now, be sure you have a good story to tell. - Amal Clooney

How wild it was, to let it be. – Cheryl Strayed

Success is not fatal; failure is not fatal: it is the courage to continue that counts. - Winston Churchill

Next time you're stressed, take a step back, inhale and laugh. Remember who you are and why you're here. You're never given anything in the world that you can't handle it. Be strong, be flexible, love yourself, and love others. Always remember, just keep moving forward. - Sharan Kaur

You define your own life. Don't let other people write your script. - Oprah Winfrey

. . .

You are never too old to set another goal or to dream a new dream. - Malala Yousafzai

At the end of the day, whether or not those people are comfortable with how you're living your life doesn't matter. What matters is whether you're comfortable with it. - Dr. Phil

People tell you the world looks a certain way. Parents tell you how to think. Schools tell you how to think. TV. Religion. And then at a certain point, if you're lucky, you realize you can make up your own mind. Nobody sets the rules but you. You can design your own life. - Carrie Ann Moss

For me, becoming isn't about arriving somewhere or achieving a certain aim. I see it instead as forward motion, a means of evolving, a way to reach continuously toward a better self. The journey doesn't end. - Michelle Obama

Remember what you have seen, because everything forgotten returns to the circling winds. – Navajo Wind Chant

He who obtains has little; he who scatters has much. - Lao Tse

People are always blaming their circumstances for what they are. I don't believe in circumstances. The people who get on in the world are the people who get up and look for the circumstances they want and if they can't find them, they make them. – George Bernard Shaw

. . .

Spread love everywhere you go. - Mother Teresa

Do not allow people to dim your shine because they are blinded. Tell them to put some sunglasses on. - Lady Gaga

If you make your internal life a priority, then everything else you need on the outside will be given to you and it will be extremely clear what the next step is. - Gabrielle Bernstein

You don't always need a plan. Sometimes you just need to breathe, trust, let go and see what happens. - Mandy Hale

Some pains have the potential to make us stronger, and some pleasures to harm us. – Donald Roberson.

Just because you took longer than others, doesn't mean you failed. I started KFC at 65. – Colonel Harland Sander

Sometimes you find exactly what you're, where looking for before you even realized you were looking for it. Stay open. Stay positive. Things can change overnight. - Doe Zantamata

Forging people in silence and never talking to them again is a form of self-care. - Denzel Washington

I fear not the man who practiced 10000 kicks once, but I fear the man who has practice one kick 10000 times. - Bruce Lee

. . .

I am okay with being a 'Loner' and having a 'Small Circle'. I enjoy my own company and only want to be around people who genuinely enjoy me. - Keanu Reeves

You can be everything. You can be the infinite number of things that people are. - Kesha

What lies behind you and what lies in front of you, pales in comparison to what lies inside of you. - Ralph Waldo Emerson

I want to be in the arena. I want to be brave with my life. And when we make the choice to dare greatly, we sign up to get our asses kicked. We can choose courage or we can choose comfort, but we can't have both. Not at the same time. - Brene Brown

I'm going to be gone one day, and I have to accept that tomorrow isn't promised. Am I OK with how I'm living today? It's the only thing I can help. If I didn't have another one, what have I done with all my todays? Am I doing a good job? - Hayley Williams

I am experienced enough to do this. I am knowledgeable enough to do this. I am prepared enough to do this. I am mature enough to do this. I am brave enough to do this. - Alexandria Ocasio-Cortez

Belief creates the actual fact. - William James

. . .

No matter what people tell you; words and ideas can change the world. - Robin Williams

I'm not going to continue knocking that old door that doesn't open for me. I'm going to create my own door and walk through that. - Ava DuVernay

It is during our darkest moments that we must focus to see the light. - Aristotle

Not having the best situation, but seeing the best in your situation is the key to happiness. - Marie Forleo

Believe you can and you're halfway there. – Theodore Roosevelt

Weaknesses are just strengths in the wrong environment. - Marianne Cantwell

Just don't give up trying to do what you really want to do. Where there is love and inspiration, I don't think you can go wrong. - Ella Fitzgerald

Silence is the last thing the world will ever hear from me. - Marlee Matlin

In a gentle way, you can shake the world. - Mahatma Gandhi

. . .

Learning how to be still, to really be still and let life happen-that stillness becomes a radiance. - Morgan Freeman

Try to be a rainbow in someone's cloud. - Maya Angelou

Everyone has inside of him a piece of good news. The good news is that you don't know how great you can be! How much you can love! What you can accomplish! And what your potential is! - Anne Frank

All you need is the plan, the road map, and the courage to press on to your destination. - Earl Nightingale

If you have good thoughts they will shine out of your face like sunbeams and you will always look lovely. - Roald Dahl

We must let go of the life we have planned, so as to accept the one that is waiting for us. - Joseph Campbell

Find out who you are and be that person. That's what your soul was put on this earth to be. Find that truth, live that truth, and everything else will come. - Ellen DeGeneres

I failed in some subjects in exam, but my friend passed in all. Now he is an engineer in Microsoft and I am the owner of Microsoft. – Bill Gates

. . .

Your journey will be much lighter and easier if you don't carry your past with you. – Brigette Nicole

You never know how strong you are until being strong is the only choice you have. – Bob Marley

Nothing is impossible to him who will try. - Alexander the Great

If you want rainbow, you have t deal with the rain. - Augustus

Don't gain the world and lose your soul, wisdom is better than silver or gold. – Bob Marley

Remember to keep balance. Life is about balance. Be kind, but don't let people abuse you. Trust, but don't be deceived. Be content, but never stop improving yourself. – Zig Ziglar

Love the life you live. Live the life you love. – Bob Marley

Silence is better than unmeaning words. – Pythagoras

I used to think that the worst think in life was to end up alone. It's not. The worst thing in life is to end up with people who make you feel alone. – Robin Williams

. . .

The best thing about the future is that it comes one day at a time. – Abraham Lincoln

Sometimes even to live is an act of courage. - Seneca

The good times of today are the sad thoughts of tomorrow. – Bob Marley

Real change, enduring change, happens one step at a time. - Ruth Bader Ginsburg

Sometimes you have to keep your good news to yourself. Everybody is not genuinely happy for you. – Von Diesel

Wake up determined, go to bed satisfied. - Dwayne "The Rock" Johnson

The true man is revealed in difficult times. - Epictetus

While we wait for life, life passes. - Seneca

Nobody built like you, you design yourself. - Jay-Z

The happiness of your life depends upon the quality of your thoughts. – Marcus Aurelius

. . .

It may see difficult at first but everything is difficult at first. – Miyamoto Musashi

You gain strength, courage, and confidence by every experience in which you really stop to look fear in the face. You are able to say to yourself, 'I lived through this horror. I can take the next thing that comes along.' You must do the thing you think you cannot do. - Eleanor Roosevelt

Know how to listen and you will profit even on those who talk badly. - Plutarch

I tell myself, 'You've been through so much, you've endured so much, time will allow me to heal, and soon this will be just another memory that made me the strong woman, athlete, and mother I am today. - Serena Williams

Acknowledging the good that you already have in your life is the foundation for all abundance. - Ralp Marsten

Live your beliefs and you can turn the world around. - Henry David Thoreau

Our lives are stories in which we write, direct and star in the leading role. Some chapters are happy while others bring lessons to learn, but we always have the power to be the heroes of our own adventures. - Joelle Speranza

. . .

Cherish the friend who tells you a harsh true, wanting ten times more to tell you a love lie. – Robert Brent

Desires make slaves out of kings and patience makes kings out of slaves. – Al Ghazali

Art is to console those who are broken by life. – Van Gogh

Life is like riding a bicycle. To keep your balance, you must keep moving. - Albert Einstein

Everything is excellent id difficult as it is rare. – Spinoza

Love all, trust a few, do wrong to none. – Shakespear

Falling down is not a failure. Failure comes when toy stay where you have fallen. - Socrates

Don't try to lessen yourself for the world; let the world catch up to you. - Beyoncé

Failure is a word unknown to me. - M. Ali Jinnah

Faith is love taking the form of aspiration. - William Ellery Channing

. . .

It is the mark of an educated mind to be able to entertain a thought without accepting it. - Aristotle

If you have a garden and a library, you have everything you need. - Cicero

When it comes to luck, you make your own. - Bruce Springsteen

Whatever you are, be a good one. - Abraham Lincoln

The limit is bot the sky, the limit is the mind. – Wim Hoff

If you don't like the road you're walking, start paving another one! - Dolly Parton

It is not that I am mad, it is only that my head is different than yours. - Diogenes

One of the hardest lessons in life is letting go whether it is guilt, anger, love, loss, or betrayal. Change is never easy. We fight to hold on and we fight to let go. – Mareez Rcys

I have learned over the years that when one's mind is made up, this diminishes fear; knowing what must be done does away with fear. - Rosa Parks

· · ·

The moral of my story is the sun always comes out after the storm. Being optimistic and surrounding yourself with positive loving people is for me, living life on the sunny side of the street. - Janice Dean

We generate fears while we sit. We overcome them by action. - Dr. Henry Link

Dreams don't have to just be dreams. You can make it a reality; if you just keep pushing and keep trying, then eventually you'll reach your goal. And if that takes a few years, then that's great, but if it takes 10 or 20, then that's part of the process. - Naomi Osaka

We are not our best intentions. We are what we do. - Amy Dickinson

I don't want anyone to walk in my shoes or walk the same path in life I have. I've learned lessons that I wouldn't wish anyone. - Akatanka

Every time you got upset at something, ask yourself if you were tomorrow, was it worth wasting your time being angry? - Robert Tew

We don't walk away to teach people a lesson. We walk away because we finally learned ours. – Dolly Parton

. . .

Do me this favor. I won't forget it. Ask your friends in the neighborhood about me. They'll tell you I know how to return a favor. -Vito Corleone

Ambition is the path to success. Persistence is the vehicle you arrive in. – Bill Brandley

Every day may not be good. But there is something good in every day. - Alice Morse Earl

I'm not upset that you lied to me, I'm upset that from now on I can't believe you. - Nietzsche

The best thing about the future is that it comes one day at a time. - Abraham Lincon

Never speak from a place of hate, jealousy, anger, or insecurity. Evaluate your words before you let them leave your lips. Sometimes it's best to be quiet. - Joey Ferrari

If you went back and fixed all the mistakes you've made, you erase yourself. - Louis C.K.

People cry, not because they are weak. It is because they've been strong for too long. - Jonny Depp

. . .

Sometimes you have to give up on people. Not because you don't care, but because they don't - Jennifer Green

If you have to talk to more than three people about the same people, then you don't want help, you want attention. -Angelina Joly

I don't chase after people anymore. If they like spending time with me, they will do so. If not, I'm content in my own company. - Barry M. Sherbal

I'm stronger because I had to be. I'm smarter because of my mistakes. Happier because of my sadness I've known and now wiser because I learned. - Barry M. Sherbal

I smile because I have survived everything the world has thrown at me. I smile because when I was knocked down, I got back up. - Barry M. Sherbal

I believe that everything happens for a reason. People change that you learn to let go, sometimes things happen to us that we just don't understand. These things sometimes become the doors and windows to our destiny. - Andrea Nugent

Things go wrong. So, that you appreciate then when they're right, you believe lies, so you eventually learn to trust no one, but yourself, and sometimes good things fall apart, so better things can fall together. -Marilyn Monroe

. . .

Forging people in silence and never talking to them again is a form of self-care. - Denzel Washington

I fear not the man who practiced 10000 kicks once, but I fear the man who has practice one kick 10000 times. - Bruce Lee

I am okay with being a 'Loner' and having a 'Small Circle'. I enjoy my own company and only want to be around people who genuinely enjoy me. - Keanu Reeves

Good things come to those who believe, better things come to those who are patient and the best things come to those who don't give up. – Milly Stone

When you feel powerless, that's because you stopped listening to your heart, that's where the power comes from. - Gianni Crow

Don't let the behavior of others destroy your inner peace. - Dalai Lama

The mind is everything. What you think, you become. - Buddha.

Pause before judging. Pause before accusing. Pause before assuming. Pause whenever you're about to react harshly, and you'll avoid doing and saying things you will regret later. - Lori Deschene

Own the morning. - Marcus Aurelius

. . .

Focus on effort, not results. - Marcus Aurelius

Read every day. – Seneca

Seek out challenges. – Seneca

Value time more than money/possessions. – Seneca

Stick with yourself, tolerant with others. – Marcus Aurelius

Meditate on your molarity daily. – Seneca

We suffer more than reality. – Seneca

It's never too late to be what you might have been. – George Elliot

Our life is what our thoughts make it. - Marcus Aurelius

The mind is everything. What you think, you become. - Buddha

I have learned that people will forget what you've said. People forget what you did. But people will never forget how you them feel. - Maya Angelou

. . .

The meaning of life is to find your gift. The purpose of life is to give it away. - Pablo Picasso

A bird does not sing because it has an answer. He sings because it has a song. - Joan Aknglund

Yu will never reach your destination, if you stop and throw stones at every dog that barks. - Winston Churchill

Don't be afraid to start again. This time, you're not starting from scratch, you're starting from experience. - Peter Hayden Dinklage

Cara about what others people think and you always be their prisoner. - Lao Tsu

Thinking is more difficult, that's why most people judge. – Carl Young

A fool is known by speech and wise man by silence. – Pythagoras

If you are the smartest person in the room, you are in the wrong room. - Confucius

The quieter you become the more you able to hear. - Rumi

. . .

Sometimes life will kick you around, but sooner or later, you realize you're not a survivor. You're a warrior, and you're stronger than anything life throws your way. - Brooks Davis

Go out into the world with your passion and love for what you do, and just never give up. - Dianne Reeve

The world will ask who you are, and if you do not know, the world will tell you. - Carl Jung

When people walk away from you, let them go. Your destiny is never tied to anyone who leaves you, and it doesn't mean they are bad people. It just means their part in your story is over. -T.D. Jakes

When you know what a man wants you know who he is and how to move him. – Petyr Baelish

Don't force yourself to fit in where you don't belong. - Tiffany M. Hart

Success consists of going from failure to failure without loss of enthusiasm. - Winston Churchill

Never forget what you are. The rest of the world will not. Wear it like armor, and it can never be used to hurt you. -Tyrion Lannister

. . .

A man with no motive is a man no one suspects. Always keep your foes confused. If they are never certain who you are or what you want, they cannon know what you are likely to do next. - Pentyl Baelish

Failure is a part of life. If you don't fail, you don't learn. If you don't learn, you'll never change. - Morgan Freeman

When a person responds to the joys and sorrows of others as if they were his own, he has attained the highest state of spiritual union. - Bhagavad Gite

Never waste your time trying to explain yourself to people who are committed to misunderstanding you. - Lil Wayne Feat

Someone once told me, "Only the people who care about you can hear you when you're quiet" and that hit me hard. – Milly Stone.

A bird sitting on a tree is never afraid of the branch breaking, because its trust is not on the branch but on its own wing. Always believe in yourself. – Milly Stone

The purpose of our lives is to be happy. - Dalai Lama

Curiosity about life in all of its aspects, I think, is still the secret of great creative people. - Leo Burnett

. . .

Life is not a problem to be solved, but a reality to be experienced. - Soren Kierkegaard

The unexamined life is not worth living. - Socrates

There is nothing permanent except change. - Heraclitus

Turn your wounds into wisdom. - Oprah Winfrey

The way I see it, if you want the rainbow, you got to put up with the rain. - Dolly Parton

Do all the good you can, for all the people you can, in all the ways you can, as long as you can. - Hillary Clinton

Don't settle for what life gives you; make life better and build something. - Ashton Kutcher

Everybody wants to be famous, but nobody wants to do the work. I live by that. You grind hard so you can play hard. At the end of the day, you put all the work in, and eventually it'll pay off. It could be in a year; it could be in 30 years. Eventually, your hard work will pay off. - Kevin Hart

Everything negative – pressure, challenges – is all an opportunity for me to rise. - Kobe Bryant

. . .

I like criticism. It makes you strong. - LeBron James

You never really learn much from hearing yourself speak. - George Clooney

Life imposes things on you that you can't control, but you still have the choice of how you're going to live through this. - Celine Dion

Life is never easy. There is work to be done and obligations to be met obligations to truth, to justice, and to liberty. - John F. Kennedy

Live for each second without hesitation. - Elton John

Life is like riding a bicycle. To keep your balance, you must keep moving. - Albert Einstein

What the superior man seeks is in himself; what the small man seeks is in others. - Confucius

Moral excellence comes about as a result of habit. We become just by doing just acts, temperate by doing temperate acts, brave by doing brave acts. - Aristotle

Life is a succession of lessons which must be lived to be understood. - Helen Keller

. . .

Your work is going to fill a large part of your life, and the only way to be truly satisfied is to do what you believe is great work. And the only way to do great work is to love what you do. If you haven't found it yet, keep looking. Don't settle. As with all matters of the heart, you'll know when you find it. - Steve Jobs

Character is destiny. - Heraclitus

My mama always said, life is like a box of chocolates. You never know what you're going to get. - Forrest Gump

Watch your thoughts; they become words. Watch your words; they become actions. Watch your actions; they become habits. Watch your habits; they become character. Watch your character; it becomes your destiny. - Lao-Tze

When we do the best, we can, we never know what miracle is wrought in our life or the life of another. - Helen Keller

The healthiest response to life is joy. - Deepak Chopra

Life is like a coin. You can spend it any way you wish, but you only spend it once. - Lillian Dickson

The best portion of a good man's life is his little nameless, unencumbered acts of kindness and of love. - Wordsworth

. . .

In three words I can sum up everything I've learned about life: It goes on. - Robert Frost

Life is ten percent what happens to you and ninety percent how you respond to it. - Charles Swindoll

Keep calm and carry on. - Winston Churchill

Life is really simple, but men insist on making it complicated. - Confucius

Maybe that's what life is a wink of the eye and winking stars. - Jack Kerouac

Life is a flower of which love is the honey. - Victor Hugo

Keep smiling, because life is a beautiful thing and there's so much to smile about. - Marilyn Monroe

Health is the greatest gift, contentment the greatest wealth, faithfulness the best relationship. - Buddha

You have brains in your head. You have feet in your shoes. You can steer yourself any direction you choose. - Dr. Seuss

. . .

Good friends, good books, and a sleepy conscience: this is the ideal life. - Mark Twain

You will never do anything in this world without courage. It is the greatest quality of the mind next to honor. - Aristotle

Life would be tragic if it weren't funny. - Stephen Hawking

Live in the sunshine, swim the sea, drink the wild air. - Ralph Waldo Emerson

The greatest pleasure of life is love. - Euripides

Life is what we make it, always has been, always will be. - Grandma Moses

Life's tragedy is that we get old too soon and wise too late. - Benjamin Franklin

Life is about making an impact, not making an income. - Kevin Kruse

I've missed more than 9000 shots in my career. I've lost almost 300 games. 26 times I've been trusted to take the game winning shot and missed. I've failed over and over and over again in my life. And that is why I succeed. - Michael Jordan

. . .

The longer I live, the more beautiful life becomes. - Frank Lloyd Wright

Every moment is a fresh beginning. - T.S. Eliot

When you cease to dream you cease to live. - Malcolm Forbes

If you spend your whole life waiting for the storm, you'll never enjoy the sunshine. - Morris West

Don't cry because it's over, smile because it happened. - Dr. Seuss

If you can do what you do best and be happy, you're further along in life than most people. - Leonardo DiCaprio

We should remember that just as a positive outlook on life can promote good health, so can everyday acts of kindness. - Hillary Clinton

Don't limit yourself. Many people limit themselves to what they think they can do. You can go as far as your mind lets you. What you believe, remember, you can achieve. - Mary Kay Ash

It is our choices that show what we truly are, far more than our abilities. - J. K. Rowling

. . .

If you're not stubborn, you'll give up on experiments too soon. And if you're not flexible, you'll pound your head against the wall and you won't see a different solution to a problem you're trying to solve. - Jeff Bezos

The best way to predict your future is to create it. - Abraham Lincoln

You must expect great things of yourself before you can do them. - Michael Jordan

Identity is a prison you can never escape, but the way to redeem your past is not to run from it, but to try to understand it, and use it as a foundation to grow. - Jay-Z

There are no mistakes, only opportunities. Tina Fey

It takes 20 years to build a reputation and five minutes to ruin it. If you think about that, you'll do things differently. - Warren Buffett

As you grow older, you will discover that you have two hands, one for helping yourself, the other for helping others. - Audrey Hepburn

Sometimes you can't see yourself clearly until you see yourself through the eyes of others. - Ellen DeGeneres

. . .

You must not lose faith in humanity. Humanity is an ocean; if a few drops of the ocean are dirty, the ocean does not become dirty. - Mahatma Gandhi

All life is an experiment. The more experiments you make, the better. - Ralph Waldo Emerson

Here's to the crazy ones, the misfits, the rebels, the troublemakers, the round pegs in the square holes the ones who see things differently they're not fond of rules' You can quote them, disagree with them, glorify or vilify them, but the only thing you can't do is ignore them because they change things. They push the human race forward, and while some may see them as the crazy ones, we see genius. - Steve Jobs

It had long since come to my attention that people of accomplishment rarely sat back and let things happen to them. They went out and happened to things. - Leonardo Da Vinci

Throughout life people will make you mad, disrespect you and treat you bad. Let God deal with the things they do, cause hate in your heart will consume you too. - Will Smith

Do not dwell in the past, do not dream of the future, concentrate the mind on the present moment. - Buddha

Life is a dream for the wise, a game for the fool, a comedy for the rich, a tragedy for the poor. - Sholom Aleichem

. . .

If you love life, don't waste time, for time is what life is made up of.
- Bruce Lee

When one door closes, another opens; but we often look so long and so regretfully upon the closed door that we do not see the one that has opened for us. - Alexander Graham Bell

Be happy for this moment. This moment is your life. - Omar Khayyam

Happiness is the feeling that power increases — that resistance is being overcome. - Friedrich Nietzsche

I have learned to seek my happiness by limiting my desires, rather than in attempting to satisfy them. - John Stuart Mill

The secret of happiness, you see is not found in seeking more, but in developing the capacity to enjoy less. - Socrates

The more man meditates upon good thoughts, the better will be his world and the world at large. - Confucius

The greatest blessings of mankind are within us and within our reach. A wise man is content with his lot, whatever it may be, without wishing for what he has not. - Seneca

.   .   .

Happiness is like a butterfly; the more you chase it, the more it will elude you, but if you turn your attention to other things, it will come and sit softly on your shoulder. - Henry David Thoreau

When it is obvious that goals can't be reached, don't adjust the goals, but adjust the action steps. - Confucius

There may be people who have more talent than you, but there's no excuse for anyone to work harder than you do – and I believe that. - Derek Jeter

Don't be afraid to fail. It's not the end of the world, and in many ways, it's the first step toward learning something and getting better at it. - Jon Hamm

Life is very interesting... in the end, some of your greatest pains, become your greatest strengths. - Drew Barrymore

I think if you live in a black-and-white world, you're going to suffer a lot. I used to be like that. But I don't believe that anymore. - Bradley Cooper

I don't believe in happy endings, but I do believe in happy travels, because ultimately, you die at a very young age, or you live long enough to watch your friends die. It's a mean thing, life. - George Clooney

. . .

It's never too late, never too late to start over, never too late to be happy. Jane Fonda

You're only human. You live once and life is wonderful, so eat the damned red velvet cupcake. - Emma Stone

A lot of people give up just before they're about to make it. You know you never know when that next obstacle is going to be the last one. - Chuck Norris

Be nice to people on the way up, because you may meet them on the way down. - Jimmy Durante

The minute that you're not learning I believe you're dead. - Jack Nicholson

Life's tough, but it's tougher when you're stupid. - John Wayne

I believe you make your day. You make your life. So much of it is all perception, and this is the form that I built for myself. I have to accept it and work within those compounds, and it's up to me. - Brad Pitt

Take up one idea. Make that one idea your life — think of it, dream of it, live on that idea. Let the brain, muscles, nerves, every part of your body be full of that idea, and just leave every other idea alone. This is the way to success. - Swami Vivekananda

. . .

I guess it comes down to a simple choice, really. Get busy living or get busy dying. - Shawshank Redemption

When we strive to become better than we are, everything around us becomes better too. - Paulo Coelho

There are three things you can do with your life: You can waste it, you can spend it, or you can invest it. The best use of your life is to invest it in something that will last longer than your time on Earth. - Rick Warren

You only pass through this life once; you don't come back for an encore. - Elvis Presley

In the long run, the sharpest weapon of all is a kind and gentle spirit. - Anne Frank

You're not defined by your past; you're prepared by it. You're stronger, more experienced, and you have greater confidence. - Joel Osteen

We become not a melting pot but a beautiful mosaic. Different people, different beliefs, different yearnings, different hopes, different dreams. - Jimmy Carter

Nothing is more honorable than a grateful heart. - Seneca

. . .

Once you figure out who you are and what you love about yourself, I think it all kind of falls into place. - Jennifer Aniston

Happy is the man who can make a living by his hobby. - George Bernard Shaw

Just disconnect. Once in a day sometime, sit silently and from all connections disconnect yourself. - Yoda

Be where you are; otherwise, you will miss your life. - Buddha

Living an experience, a particular fate, is accepting it fully. - Albert Camus

The more you praise and celebrate your life, the more there is in life to celebrate. - Oprah Winfrey

Your image isn't your character. Character is what you are as a person. - Derek Jeter

Football is like life, it requires perseverance, self-denial, hard work sacrifice, dedication and respect for authority. - Vince Lombardi

As you know, life is an echo; we get what we give. - David DeNotaris

There are no regrets in life, just lessons. - Jennifer Aniston

. . .

I believe that nothing in life is unimportant every moment can be a beginning. - John McLeod

Find people who will make you better. - Michelle Obama

As my knowledge of things grew, I felt more and more the delight of the world I was in. - Helen Keller

Benjamin Franklin was a humanitarian that dedicated his life to making contributions to all humans. He had a clear purpose for himself: improve the human race. - Paulo Braga

Don't allow your past or present condition to control you. It's just a process that you're going through to get you to the next level. - T.D. Jakes

My mission in life is not merely to survive, but to thrive; and to do so with some passion, some compassion, some humor, and some style. - Maya Angelou

If we don't change, we don't grow. If we don't grow, we aren't really living. - Gail Sheehy

You choose the life you live. If you don't like it, it's on you to change it because no one else is going to do it for you. - Kim Kiyosaki

. . .

Life doesn't require that we be the best, only that we try our best. - H. Jackson Brown Jr.

The way I see it, every life is a pile of good things and bad things. The good things don't always soften the bad things, but vice versa, the bad things don't always spoil the good things and make them unimportant. - Doctor Who

Success doesn't come from occasional bouts of inspiration and passion. It comes from putting in excellent work day in and day out. - Aristotle

Life isn't about waiting for the storm to pass; it's about learning to dance in the rain. - Vivian Greene

I enjoy life when things are happening. I don't care if it's good things or bad things. That means you're alive. - Joan Rivers

There's more to life than basketball. The most important thing is your family and taking care of each other and loving each other no matter what. - Stephen Curry

Today, you have 100% of your life left. - Tom Landry

Nobody who ever gave his best regretted it. - George Halas

. . .

Make each day your masterpiece. - John Wooden

You can't put a limit on anything. The more you dream, the farther you get. - Michael Phelps

Sometimes you have to keep your good news to yourself. Everybody is not genuinely happy for you. - Vin Diesel

I used to think that the worst thing in life was to end up alone. It's not. The worst thing in life is to end up with people who make you feel alone. - Robin Williams

The best thing about the future is that it comes one day at a time. - Abraham Lincoln

Mora experience comes about as a result of a habit. - Plato

Remember to keep your balance. Life is about balance. Be kind, but don't let people abuse you. Trust, but don't be deceived. Be content, but never stop improving yourself. - Zig Ziglar

The happiest of your life depends upon the quality of your thoughts. - Marcus Aurelius

We are what we repeatedly do. Excellence, then, is not an act, but a habit. - Aristotle

. . .

While we wait for life, life passes. - Seneca

Sometimes even to live is an act of courage. - Seneca

It may see difficult at first, but everything is difficult at first. - Miyamoto Musashi

The true man is revealed in difficult times. - Epictetus

Silence is better than unmeaning words. - Pythagoras

Good humor is one of the best articles of dress one can wear in society. - William Makepeace Tackery

It's fine to celebrate success but it is more important to heed the lessons of failure. - Bill Gate.

Don't count days, make the days count. - Muhammad Ali

There is nothing more lonely that being surrounded with a room of people that have nothing in common with. - Ari Rastegar

Pleasure in the job puts perfection in the work. - Aristotle

. . .

Life is going to test you every single day not to punish you, but to train you to have strength for another day and guide you to become the warrior that your sere mean to be. – Roger Lee

A person who never made a mistake never tried anything new. - Albert Einstein

The best way to predict the future is to create it. - Abraham Lincoln

Nothing is impossible. The word itself say "I'm possible." - Audrey Hepburn

We work to become, not to acquire. - Elbert Hubbard

Your time is limited. Don't waste it living someone else's life. - Steve Jobs

You can't use up creativity. The more you use, the more you have. - Maya Angelou

Acknowledging the good that you already have in your life is the foundation for all abundance. - Ralph Marsten

Good humor is one of the best articles of dress one can wear in society. - William Makepeace Thackery

. . .

Good people do not need laws to tell them to act responsibly, while bad people will find a way around the laws. - Plato

You do not find the happy life. You make it. – Camellia Eyring Kimball

We need to take risks. We need to go broke. We need to prove them wrong. Simply by not giving up. – Awkwafina

Faith is love taking the form of aspiration. – William Ellery Channing

Never discourage anyone who continually makes progress, no matter how slow. - Plato.

When you seen beyond yourself, then you may find peace of mind is waiting for you. – George Harrison

Out of the mountain of despair, a stone of hope. - Martin Luther King Jr

I tell myself, 'You've been through so much, you've endured so much, time will allow me to heal, and soon this will be just another memory that made me the strong woman, athlete and mother, I am today.' - Seneca Williams

In a gentle way, you can shake the world. – Mahatma Gandhi

. . .

Learning how to be still, to really be still and let life happen that stillness becomes a radiance. – Morgan Freeman

Sex in the body is fine, Money in the pocket is fine, they only become when they enter your mind. - Izzamuzzic Polozhenie

Everyone has inside of him/or her a piece of good news. The good news is that you don't know how great you can be. How much you can love, what you can accomplish. And what your potential s. – Anne Frank

Wise men speak because they have something to say, fools because they have to say something. - Plato

All you need is the plan, the road map and the courage to press on to your destination. – Earl Nightingale

If you have good thoughts, they will shine out of your face like sunbeams and you will always look lovely. – Roald Dahl

Try to be a rainbow in someone's life. Maya Angelou

Just don't give up trying t do what you really want to do. Where there is love and inspiration, I don't think you can go wrong. – Ella Fitzerald

. . .

Weaknesses are just strengths in the wrong environment. – Marriane Cantwell

Believe you can and you're half way there. Theodore Rosevelt

You can easily forgive a child who is afraid of the dark. We do not act rightly because we are excellent in fact, we achieve excellence by acting rightly. - Plato

It's important for those who have done certain things to keep or giving because it's part of the progress of how life recycles and brings new generation forward. - Stefanos Tsitsipas

Coffee knew it will taste nice and sweet, before it met sugar and milk. We are good as individuals but become better when we blend with the right people. - Denis Agaba

When someone is mean, don't listen. When someone is rude, walk away. When someone tries to put you down, stay firm. Don't let someone else's behavior destroy your inner peace. - Dennis Agaba

You will never do anything in this world without courage. - Plato

Most of the important things in the world have been accomplished by people who have kept trying when there seemed no hope at all. - Dale Carnegie

. . .

Life is going to test you every single day not to punish you but to train you to have strength for another day and guide you to become the warrior that you were meant to be. - Roger Lee

Life has knocked me down a few times. It has shown me things I never wanted to see. I have experienced sadness and failures, but one thing for sure I always get up. - Scott Calum

To be the best, you must be able to handle the worst. - Dennis Agaba

Sometimes people pretend you're bad person, so they don't feel guilty about the things they did to you. - Denis Agaba

A time will come in your life where some people will regret why they treated you wrong. Trust me it will definitely come. - Mr. Wise

I found peace the day I told myself that everything happens for a reason. And everything has its own time. - John David

You can't go back and change the beginning, but you can start where you are and Care abuts what other people think and you will always be throat prisoner. - Lao Tsu

Ther fool id known by speech and the wise man by silence. - Pythagoras

. . .

If you are the smartest person in the room, you're in the wrong room. – Confucius

The quitter you become, the more you are able to hear. – Rumi

Try to accomplish things you have always dreamed of while you can. I know it sounds chiche, but the biggest lesson I have learned is that life is precious; enjoy it while it last. - Lisa Ling

There are going to be times where you're pushed down and have to get up again. Having that kind of an attitude helps you gain a clearer picture of things. The way I approach life, the way I see those values that I want to be linked to in life. These are values that are extremely important to have. Whatever you give, you get back. - Stefanos Tsitsipas

Insults are the last results of insecure people with a crumbling position trying to appear confident. - Path Tumbla

Stop offering the hand if it is not taken. If you, then stop 're trying to help and it doesn't work, stop helping. If you're offering something and it's not taken, you have to stop offering the hand, because then is no other solution. If someone who is sinking and has his hands around your neck and is pulling you down, you are not obligated to drown with them. And sometimes that means in people's lives, for example, if they have to leave their family members behind. Now there is a rule if you're a lifeguard. I'll save you, but that doesn't mean you to drawn me, while I am doing it. And if it's you drown, it is you drown. And that is wisdom. That's not cruelty. – Morgan Freeman

. . .

No one has the power to take your happiness unless you give it to them. - Dr. Amaka Nwaza

Never refriend a person that has tried to destroy your character, your money or your relationships. A snake only sheds its skin to become a bigger snake. - George Clooney

You will never understand the damage you did to someone until the same thing is done to you. That's why I am here. - Karma

If you have been brutally broken, but still have the courage to be gentle to others then you deserve a love deeper than the ocean itself. -Nikita Gill

We are what we repeatedly do. - Plato

The most dangerous person is one who listens, thinks, and observes. -Bruce Lee

No one is coming. No one. No one is coming to push you. No one is coming to tell you to turn the TV off. No one is coming to tell you to get out the door and exercise. Nobody is coming to tell you to apply for that job. You've always dream about. Nobody is coming to write the business plan for you. It's up to you. And because you're only ever going to the things that you feel like doing right now, or that feel good right now. Unless you understand that you've got to parent yourself, you got to push yourself, you're not going to make your dreams come true. – Morgan Freeman

Positive anything is better than negative nothing. - Elbert Hubbard

Miracles happen to those who believe in them. - Bernhard Berenson

One small positive thought can change your whole day. - Zig Ziglar

Believe you can and you're halfway there. - Teddy Roosevelt

Be positive. Be true. Be kind. - Roy T. Bennett

You cannot have a positive life and a negative mind. - Joyce Meyer

If you are positive, you'll see opportunities instead of obstacles. - Widad Akrawi

Write it on your heart that every day is the best day in the year. - Ralph Waldo Emerson

Accentuate the positive, Eliminate the Negative, latch onto the affirmative. - Bing Crosby

I will go anywhere as long as it's forward. - David Livingston

. . .

My dear friend, clear your mind of can't. - Samuel Johnson

Keep a smile on your face. Keep a spring in your step. - Joel Osteen

A positive atmosphere nurtures a positive attitude, which is required to take positive action. - Richard M. DeVos

Turn every life situation into a positive one. - Rhonda Byrne

The most positive men are the most credulous. - Alexander Pope

For a man to conquer himself is the first and noblest of all victories. - Plato

Believe that life is worth living and your belief will help create the fact. - William James

Your positive action combined with positive thinking results in success. - Shiv Khera

It's almost always possible to be honest and positive. - Naval Ravikant

. . .

Don't focus on negative things; focus on the positive, and you will flourish. - Alek Wek

Inspiration comes from within yourself. One has to be positive. When you're positive, good things happen. - Deep Roy

Surround yourself with positive people and you'll be a positive person. - Kellie Pickler

Virtually nothing is impossible in this world if you just put your mind to it and maintain a positive attitude. - Lou Holtz

It's most important that you surround yourself with positivity always, and have it in your mind at all times. - Tyler Perry

When you are joyful, when you say yes to life and have fun and project positivity all around you, you become a sun in the center of every constellation, and people want to be near you. - Shannon L. Alder

In every day, there are 1,440 minutes. That means we have 1,440 daily opportunities to make a positive impact. - Les Brown

I surround myself with positive, productive people of good will and decency. - Ted Nugent

. . .

The three 'C's' of leadership are: 1. Consideration; 2 caring, and 3. courtesy. Be polite to everyone. – Brian Tracy

The words of all deceptions are self-deception. - Plato

There is no advertisement as powerful as a positive reputation traveling fast. - Brian Koslow

The less you respond to negative people, the more positive your life will become. - Paolo Coelho

Change your thoughts and you change your world. - Norman Vincent Peale

I believe that you should gravitate to people who are doing productive and positive things with their lives. - Nadia Comaneci

Dwell on the beauty of life. Watch the stars, and see yourself running with them. - Marcus Aurelius

The power for creating a better future is contained in the present moment: You create a good future by creating a good present. - Eckhart Tolle

Shoot for the moon. Even if you miss, you'll land among the stars. - Norman Vincent Peale

. . .

To please the many is to displease the wise. - Plutarch

The whole of life is but a moment of time. It is our duty, therefore to use it, not to misuse it. - Plutarch

The effective leader recognizes that they are more dependent on their people than they are on them. Walk softly. – Brian Tracy

Practice golden rule management in everything you do. Manage others the way you would like to be managed. – Brian Tracy

The drop hollows out the stone not by strength, but by constant falling. - Plutarch

The true test of leadership is how well you function in a crisis. - Brian Tracy

Respect is the key determinant of high-performance leadership. How much people respect you determines how well they perform. – Brian Tracy

We can complain because rose bushes have thorns, or rejoice because thorns have roses. - Alphonse Karr

Believing in negative thoughts is the single greatest obstruction to success. - Charles F. Glassman

. . .

If opportunity doesn't knock, build a door. - Milton Berle

Every day may not be good... but there's something good in every day. - Alice Morse Earle

Leaders are anticipatory thinkers. They consider all consequences of their behaviors before they act. – Brian Tracy

Live life to the fullest and focus on the positive. – Matt Cameron

In order to carry a positive action, we must develop here a positive vision. - Dalai Lama

A problem is a chance for you to do your best. - Duke Ellington

Most of the important things in the world have been accomplished by people who have kept on trying when there seemed to be no hope at all. - Dale Carnegie

There are far, far better things ahead than anything we leave behind. - C.S. Lewis

Keep looking up, that's the secret of life. – Charlie Brown

. . .

We are all in the gutter, but some of us are looking at the stars. - Oscar Wilde

You need to be able to manage stress because hard times will come, and a positive outlook is what gets you through. - Marie Osmond

You have to train your brain to be positive just like you work out your body. - Shawn Achor

Don't be pushed around by the fears in your mind. Be led by the dreams in your heart. - Roy T. Bennett

The only place where your dreams become impossible is in your own thinking. - Robert H. Shuller

Always turn a negative situation into a positive situation. – Michael Jordan

Cultivate an optimistic mind, use your imagination, always consider alternatives, and dare to believe that you can make possible what others think is impossible. - Rodolfo Costa

Positive thinking is more than just a tagline. It changes the way we behave. And I firmly believe that when I am positive, it not only makes me better, but it also makes those around me better. - Harvey Mackay

. . .

What is the difference between an obstacle and an opportunity? Our attitude toward it. Every opportunity has a difficult, and every difficulty has an opportunity. - J. Sidlow Baxter

An attitude of positive expectation is the mark of the superior personality. - Brian Tracy

Keep your face to the sunshine and you cannot see a shadow. - Helen Keller

We become what we think about. – Earl Nightingale

Once you replace negative thoughts with positive ones, you'll start having positive results. - Willie Nelson

Positive thinking will let you do everything better than negative thinking will. - Zig Ziglar

When you are enthusiastic about what you do, you feel this positive energy. It's very simple. -Paolo Coelho

It makes a big difference in your life when you stay positive. - Ellen DeGeneris

Even though you're fed up, you got to keep your head up. -Tupac Shakur

. . .

The positive thinker sees the invisible, feels the intangible, and achieves the impossible. - Winston Churchill

Positive thinking must be followed by positive doing. – John C. Maxwell

I've always believed that you can think positive just as well as you can think negative. - James Baldwin

I'm a very positive thinker, and I think that is what helps me the most in difficult moments. - Roger Federer

I think positive emotion trumps negative emotion every time. - Leonardo DiCaprio

The best is yet to be. – Robert Browning

Try to be a rainbow in someone's cloud. – Maya Angelou

A positive mindset brings positive things. – Phillip Reiter

The greatest glory in living lies not in never falling, but in rising every time we fall. - Nelson Mandela

The way to get started is to quit talking and begin doing. -Walt Disney

. . .

Your time is limited, so don't waste it living someone else's life. Don't be trapped by dogma – which is living with the results of other people's thinking. - Steve Jobs

If life were predictable it would cease to be life, and be without flavor. - Eleanor Roosevelt

If you look at what you have in life, you'll always have more. If you look at what you don't have in life, you'll never have enough. - Oprah Winfrey

If you set your goals ridiculously high and it's a failure, you will fail above everyone else's success. - James Cameron

Life is what happens when you're busy making other plans. - John Lennon

Spread love everywhere you go. Let no one ever come to you without leaving happier. - Mother Teresa

When you reach the end of your rope, tie a knot in it and hang on. - Franklin D. Roosevelt

Always remember that you are absolutely unique. Just like everyone else. - Margaret Mead

. . .

Don't judge each day by the harvest you reap but by the seeds that you plant. - Robert Louis Stevenson

The future belongs to those who believe in the beauty of their dreams. - Eleanor Roosevelt

Tell me and I forget. Teach me and I remember. Involve me and I learn. - Benjamin Franklin

The best and most beautiful things in the world cannot be seen or even touched, they must be felt with the heart. - Helen Keller

It is during our darkest moments that we must focus to see the light. - Aristotle

Whoever is happy will make others happy too. - Anne Frank

It is during our darkest moments that we must focus to see the light. - Aristotle

Whoever is happy will make others happy too. - Anne Frank

Do not go where the path may lead, go instead where there is no path and leave a trail. - Ralph Waldo Emerson

. . .

You will face many defeats in life, but never let yourself be defeated. - Maya Angelou

The greatest glory in living lies not in never falling, but in rising every time we fall. - Nelson Mandela

In the end, it's not the years in your life that count. It's the life in your years. - Abraham Lincoln

Never let the fear of striking out keep you from playing the game. - Babe Ruth

Life is either a daring adventure or nothing at all. - Helen Keller

Many of life's failures are people who did not realize how close they were to success when they gave up. -Thomas A. Edison

You have brains in your head. You have feet in your shoes. You can steer yourself any direction you choose. - Dr. Seuss

Keep smiling, because life is a beautiful thing and there's so much to smile about. - Marilyn Monroe

Life is a long lesson in humility. - James M. Barrie

. . .

In three words I can sum up everything I've learned about life: it goes on. - Robert Frost

Love the life you live. Live the life you love. - Bob Marley

Life is either a daring adventure or nothing at all. - Helen Keller

You have brains in your head. You have feet in your shoes. You can steer yourself any direction you choose. - Dr. Seuss

Life is made of ever so many partings welded together. - Charles Dickens

Your time is limited, so don't waste it living someone else's life. Don't be trapped by dogma — which is living with the results of other people's thinking. - Steve Jobs

Life is trying things to see if they work. - Ray Bradbury

Many of life's failures are people who did not realize how close they were to success when they gave up. -Thomas A. Edison

Keep smiling, because life is a beautiful thing and there's so much to smile about. - Marilyn Monroe

. . .

Success is not final; failure is not fatal: It is the courage to continue that counts. - Winston S. Churchill

Success usually comes to those who are too busy to be looking for it. - Henry David Thoreau

The way to get started is to quit talking and begin doing. - Walt Disney

If you really look closely, most overnight successes took a long time. - Steve Jobs

The secret of success is to do the common thing uncommonly well. - John D. Rockefeller Jr.

I find that the harder I work, the more luck I seem to have. -Thomas Jefferson

The real test is not whether you avoid this failure, because you won't. It's whether you let it harden or shame you into inaction, or whether you learn from it; whether you choose to persevere. - Barack Obama

Success is not final; failure is not fatal: It is the courage to continue that counts. - Winston S. Churchill

Don't be distracted by criticism. Remember the only taste of success some people get is to take a bite out of you. - Zig Ziglar

. . .

I never dreamed about success, I worked for it. - Estee Lauder

Success seems to be connected with action. Successful people keep moving. They make mistakes but they don't quit. - Conrad Hilton

There are no secrets to success. It is the result of preparation, hard work, and learning from failure. - Colin Powell

The real test is not whether you avoid this failure, because you won't. It's whether you let it harden or shame you into inaction, or whether you learn from it; whether you choose to persevere. - Barack Obama

The only limit to our realization of tomorrow will be our doubts of today. - Franklin D. Roosevelt

It is better to fail in originality than to succeed in imitation. - Herman Melville

Successful people do what unsuccessful people are not willing to do. Don't wish it were easier; wish you were better. - Jim Rohn

The road to success and the road to failure are almost exactly the same. - Colin R. Davis

I failed my way to success. -Thomas Edison

. . .

Leaders are never satisfied; they continually strive to be better. – Brian Tracy

A successful man is one who can lay a firm foundation with the brick's others have thrown at him. - David Brinkley

Things work out best for those who make the best of how things work out. - John Wooden

Try not to become a man of success. Rather become a man of value. - Albert Einstein

Don't be afraid to give up the good to go for the great. - John D. Rockefeller

Always bear in mind that your own resolution to success is more important than any other one thing. - Abraham Lincoln

Success is walking from failure to failure with no loss of enthusiasm. - Winston Churchill

You know you are on the road to success if you would do your job and not be paid for it. - Oprah Winfrey

If you want to achieve excellence, you can get there today. As of this second, quit doing less-than-excellent work. -Thomas J. Watson

. . .

If you genuinely want something, don't wait for it - teach yourself to be impatient. - Gurbaksh Chahal

The only place where success comes before work is in the dictionary. - Vidal Sassoon

If you are not willing to risk the usual, you will have to settle for the ordinary. - Jim Rohn

Before anything else, preparation is the key to success. - Alexander Graham Bell

People who succeed have momentum. The more they succeed, the more they want to succeed and the more they find a way to succeed. Similarly, when someone is failing, the tendency is to get on a downward spiral that can even become a self-fulfilling prophecy. - Tony Robbins

You miss 100% of the shots you don't take. - Wayne Gretzky

Whether you think you can or you think you can't, you're right. - Henry Ford

I have learned over the years that when one's mind is made up, this diminishes fear. - Rosa Parks

· · ·

I alone cannot change the world, but I can cast a stone across the water to create many ripples. - Mother Teresa

Nothing is impossible, the word itself says, 'I'm possible!' - Audrey Hepburn

The question isn't who is going to let me; it's who is going to stop me. - Ayn Rand

The only person you are destined to become is the person you decide to be. - Ralph Waldo Emerson

Believe you can and you're halfway there. -Theodore Roosevelt

The only person you are destined to become is the person you decide to be. - Ralph Waldo Emerson

I've learned that people will forget what you said, people will forget what you did, but people will never forget how you made them feel. - Maya Angelou

The question isn't who is going to let me; it's who is going to stop me. - Ayn Rand

Winning isn't everything, but wanting to win is. - Vince Lombardi

. . .

Whether you think you can or you think you can't, you're right. - Henry Ford

You miss 100% of the shots you don't take. - Wayne Gretzky

I alone cannot change the world, but I can cast a stone across the water to create many ripples. - Mother Teresa

You become what you believe. - Oprah Winfrey

The most difficult thing is the decision to act, the rest is merely tenacity. -Amelia Earhart

How wonderful it is that nobody need wait a single moment before starting to improve the world. - Anne Frank

An unexamined life is not worth living. - Socrates

Everything you've ever wanted is on the other side of fear. - George Addair

Dream big and dare to fail. - Norman Vaughan

You may be disappointed if you fail, but you are doomed if you don't try. - Beverly Sills

. . .

Life is 10% what happens to me and 90% of how I react to it. - Charles Swindoll

It does not matter how slowly you go as long as you do not stop. - Confucius

When everything seems to be going against you, remember that the airplane takes off against the wind, not with it. - Henry Ford

Too many of us are not living our dreams because we are living our fears. - Les Brown

I have learned over the years that when one's mind is made up, this diminishes fear. - Rosa Parks

I didn't fail the test. I just found 100 ways to do it wrong. - Benjamin Franklin

If you're offered a seat on a rocket ship, don't ask what seat! Just get on. - Sheryl Sandberg

I attribute my success to this: I never gave or took any excuse. - Florence Nightingale

I would rather die of passion than of boredom. -Vincent van Gogh

. . .

If you look at what you have in life, you'll always have more. If you look at what you don't have in life, you'll never have enough. - Oprah Winfrey

Dreaming, after all, is a form of planning. - Gloria Steinem

Whatever the mind of man can conceive and believe, it can achieve. - Napoleon Hill

First, have a definite, clear practical ideal; a goal, an objective. Second, have the necessary means to achieve your ends; wisdom, money, materials, and methods. Third, adjust all your means to that end. - Aristotle

Twenty years from now you will be more disappointed by the things that you didn't do than by the ones you did do. So, throw off the bowlines, sail away from safe harbor, catch the trade winds in your sails. Explore, Dream, Discover. - Mark Twain

If you want to live a happy life, tie it to a goal not to people or objects. - Albert Einstein

You will stop worrying so much what the other people think of you, when you realize how seldom they do. - David Foster Wallace

Knowledge is learning something every day. Wisdom is letting go of something every day. - Zen Proverb

. . .

The color of your skin is less important than the spirit which moves it. - Cree Nation

Sometimes when you smile, it's not because you're happy. It's because you're strong. - Pamela Anderson

Stop telling people more than they need to know. - Leonardo DiCaprio

I do not work for money. I work for the freedom. - Leonardo DiCaprio

They ignore you until they need you. Godfather – Marlo Brando

I respect a person who respects me when I'm not around. - Godfather

A person who left in anger will always come back. But the one who left with a smile will never be back again. – Edris Elba

The world is a dangerous place to live; not because of the people who are evil, but because of the people who don't do anything about it. - Albert Einstein

If you don't go after what you want, you'll never have it. If you don't ask, the answer is always no. If you don't step forward, you're always in the same place. - Nora Roberts.

. . .

The funny thing is when you don't let the people disrespect you, they start calling you difficult. - Will Smith.

We are shared by our thoughts; we become what we think. - Buddha

If you are depressed, you are living in the past. If you are anxious, you are living in the future. If you are at peace, you are living in the present. - Lao Tzu

When you talk, you're only repeating what you already know. But if you listen, you may learn something new. - Dalai Lama

It's not how hard you hit. It's how hard you get hit...and keep moving forward. - Rocky Balboa

You break your own heart by making someone more important to you than you're to them. Never play yourself like that. – Chris Hemsworth

Weak people revenge. Strong people forgive. Intelligent people ignore. - Albert Einstein

Better to die on one's feet than to live on one's knees. - Jean Paul Sartre

. . .

If you don't want to be stabbed in the back, you should be aware of who is standing behind you. -Tony Miles

Since we're all going to die, it's obvious that when and how don't matter. -Albert Camus

You can do two things at once, but you can't focus effectively on two things at once. - Gary W. Keller

Whatever you do, do it with all your heart and soul. - Bernard Barush

You only know yourself when you go beyond your limits. - Paulo Coelho

Treat your mind like your money, don't waste. - Sophia Amoroso

Life is too short. We spend so much time sweating the small stuff; worrying, complaining, gossiping, comparing, wishing, wanting, and waiting for something improved instead of focusing on all the simple blessings that surround us every day. Life is so fragile and all it takes a single moment to change everything you take for granted. Focus on what's important and be grateful. You are blessed! Believe it! live your life and leave no regrets. – Hippocrates/Benjamin Disraeli

Sad but true. 'I used to think worst thing in life was to end up alone.

It's not. The worst thing in life is to end up with people who make you feel alone.' - Robin Williams

We cannot solve problems with the kind of thinking we employed when we came up with them. - Albert Einstein

Learn as if you will live forever, live like you will die tomorrow. - Mahatma Gandhi

Stay away from those people who try to disparage your ambitions. Small minds will always do that, but great minds will give you a feeling that you can become great too. - Mark Twain

When you give joy to other people, you get more joy in return. You should give a good thought to happiness that you can give out. - Eleanor Roosevelt

When you change your thoughts, remember to also change your world. - Norman Vincent Peale

It is only when we take chances when our lives improve. The initial and the most difficult risk that we need to take is to become honest. - Walter Anderson

Nature has given us all the pieces required to achieve exceptional wellness and health but has left it to us to put these pieces together. - Diane McLaren

. . .

Success is not final; failure is not fatal: It is the courage to continue that counts. - Winston S. Churchill

It is better to fail in originality than to succeed in imitation. - Herman Melville

The road to success and the road to failure are almost exactly the same. - Colin R. Davis

Success usually comes to those who are too busy looking for it. - Henry David Thoreau

Develop success from failures. Discouragement and failure are two of the surest steppingstones to success. - Dale Carnegie

Nothing in the world can take the place of Persistence. Talent will not; nothing is more common than unsuccessful men with talent. Genius will not; unrewarded genius is almost a proverb. Education will not; the world is full of educated derelicts. The slogan 'Press On' has solved and always will solve the problems of the human race. - Calvin Coolidge

There are three ways to ultimate success: The first way is to be kind. The second way is to be kind. The third way is to be kind. - Mister Rogers

Success is peace of mind, which is a direct result of self-satisfaction in knowing you made the effort to become the best of which you are capable. - John Wooden

I never dreamed about success. I worked for it. - Estée Lauder

Success is getting what you want, happiness is wanting what you get. - W. P. Kinsella

The pessimist sees difficulty in every opportunity. The optimist sees opportunity in every difficulty. - Winston Churchill

Don't let yesterday take up too much of today. - Will Rogers

You learn more from failure than from success. Don't let it stop you. Failure builds character. - Anonymous

If you are working on something that you really care about, you don't have to be pushed. The vision pulls you. - Steve Jobs

Experience is a hard teacher because she gives the test first, the lesson afterwards. - Vernon Sanders Law

To know how much there is to know is the beginning of learning to live. - Dorothy West

Goal setting is the secret to a compelling future. - Tony Robbins

. . .

Concentrate all your thoughts upon the work in hand. The sun's rays do not burn until brought to a focus. - Alexander Graham Bell

Either you run the day, or the day runs you. - Jim Rohn

I'm a greater believer in luck, and I find the harder I work the more I have of it. - Thomas Jefferson

When we strive to become better than we are, everything around us becomes better too. - Paulo Coelho

Opportunity is missed by most people because it is dressed in overalls and looks like work. - Thomas Edison

Setting goals is the first step in turning the invisible into the visible. - Tony Robbins

Your work is going to fill a large part of your life, and the only way to be truly satisfied is to do what you believe is great work. And the only way to do great work is to love what you do. If you haven't found it yet, keep looking. Don't settle. As with all matters of the heart, you'll know when you find it. - Steve Jobs

It's not about better time management. It's about better life management. - Alexandra of The Productivity Zone

· · ·

Success is not final; failure is not fatal: It is the courage to continue that counts. - Winston S. Churchill

It is better to fail in originality than to succeed in imitation. - Herman Melville

The road to success and the road to failure are almost exactly the same. - Colin R. Davis

Success usually comes to those who are too busy looking for it. - Henry David Thoreau

Develop success from failures. Discouragement and failure are two of the surest steppingstones to success. - Dale Carnegie

There are three ways to ultimate success: The first way is to be kind. The second way is to be kind. The third way is to be kind. - Mister Rogers

Success is peace of mind, which is a direct result of self-satisfaction in knowing you made the effort to become the best of which you are capable. - John Wooden

I never dreamed about success. I worked for it. - Estée Lauder

· · ·

Success is getting what you want, happiness is wanting what you get. - W. P. Kinsella

The pessimist sees difficulty in every opportunity. The optimist sees opportunity in every difficulty. - Winston Churchill

Don't let yesterday take up too much of today. - Will Rogers

If you are working on something that you really care about, you don't have to be pushed. The vision pulls you. - Steve Jobs

Experience is a hard teacher because she gives the test first, the lesson afterwards. - Vernon Sanders Law

To know how much there is to know is the beginning of learning to live. - Dorothy West

Goal setting is the secret to a compelling future. - Tony Robbins

Concentrate all your thoughts upon the work in hand. The sun's rays do not burn until brought to a focus. - Alexander Graham Bell

Either you run the day, or the day runs you. - Jim Rohn

I'm a greater believer in luck, and I find the harder I work the more I have of it. - Thomas Jefferson

. . .

When we strive to become better than we are, everything around us becomes better too. - Paulo Coelho

Opportunity is missed by most people because it is dressed in overalls and looks like work. - Thomas Edison

Setting goals is the first step in turning the invisible into the visible. - Tony Robbins

Your work is going to fill a large part of your life, and the only way to be truly satisfied is to do what you believe is great work. And the only way to do great work is to love what you do. If you haven't found it yet, keep looking. Don't settle. As with all matters of the heart, you'll know when you find it. - Steve Jobs

It's not about better time management. It's about better life management. - Alexandra of The Productivity Zone

Women challenge the status quo because we are never it. - Cindy Gallop

We don't just sit around and wait for other people. We just make, and we do. - Arlan Hamilton

Think like a queen. A queen is not afraid to fail. Failure is another steppingstone to greatness. - Oprah Winfrey

. . .

Whenever you see a successful woman, look out for three men who are going out of their way to try to block her. - Yulia Tymoshenko

Some women choose to follow men, and some choose to follow their dreams. If you're wondering which way to go, remember that your career will never wake up and tell you that it doesn't love you anymore. - Lady Gaga

The thing women have yet to learn is nobody gives you power. You just take it. - Roseanne Barr

A witty woman is a treasure; a witty beauty is a power. - George Meredith

When a woman becomes her own best friend life is easier. - Diane Von Furstenberg

If you want something said, ask a man; if you want something done, ask a woman. - Margaret Thatcher

We need women at all levels, including the top, to change the dynamic, reshape the conversation, to make sure women's voices are heard and heeded, not overlooked and ignored. - Sheryl Sandberg

It took me quite a long time to develop a voice, and now that I have it, I am not going to be silent. - Madeleine Albright

. . .

Women must learn to play the game as men do. - Eleanor Roosevelt

I swear, by my life and my love of it, that I will never live for the sake of another man, nor ask another man to live for mine. - Ayn Rand

He who conquers himself is the mightiest warrior. - Confucius

Try not to become a man of success, but rather become a man of value. - Albert Einstein

One man with courage makes a majority. - Andrew Jackson

One secret of success in life is for a man to be ready for his opportunity when it comes. – Benjamin Disraeli

A man who has committed a mistake and doesn't correct it is committing another mistake. – Confucius Kongzi

The successful man will profit from his mistakes and try again in a different way. – Dale Carnegie

A successful man is one who can lay a firm foundation with the brick's others have thrown at him. – David Brinkley

. . .

He is a wise man who does not grieve for the things which he has not but rejoices for those which he has. – Epictetus

You've got to get up every morning with determination if you're going to go to bed with satisfaction. - George Lorimer

Education is the most powerful weapon which you can use to change the world. - Nelson Mandela

The most difficult thing is the decision to act, the rest is merely tenacity. - Amelia Earhart

You'll find that education is just about the only thing lying around loose in this world, and it's about the only thing a fellow can have as much of as he's willing to haul away. - John Graham

Take the attitude of a student, never be too big to ask questions, never know too much to learn something new. - Augustine Og Mandino

The elevator to success is out of order. You'll have to use the stairs, one step at a time. - Joe Girard

Be a positive energy trampoline – absorb what you need and rebound more back. - Dave Carolan

. . .

People often say that motivation doesn't last. Well, neither does bathing – that's why we recommend it daily. - Zig Ziglar

I am so clever that sometimes I don't understand a single word of what I am saying. - Oscar Wilde

People say nothing is impossible, but I do nothing every day. - Winnie the Pooh

Life is like a sewer what you get out of it depends on what you put into it. - Tom Lehrer

I always wanted to be somebody, but now I realize I should have been more specific. - Lily Tomlin

Talent wins games, but teamwork and intelligence win championships. - Michael Jordan

Individual commitment to a group effort that is what makes a teamwork, a company work, a society work, a civilization work. - Vince Lombardi

Teamwork is the ability to work together toward a common vision. The ability to direct individual accomplishments toward organizational objectives. It is the fuel that allows common people to attain uncommon results. - Andrew Carnegie

.   .   .

Coming together is a beginning. Keeping together is progress. Working together is success. - Henry Ford

Alone we can do so little, together we can do so much. - Helen Keller

Remember, teamwork begins by building trust. And the only way to do that is to overcome our need for invulnerability. - Patrick Lencioni

I invite everyone to choose forgiveness rather than division, teamwork over personal ambition. - Jean-Francois Cope

Just one small positive thought in the morning can change your whole day. - Dalai Lama

Opportunities don't happen, you create them. - Chris Grosser

Love your family, work super hard, live your passion. - Gary Vaynerchuk

It is never too late to be what you might have been. - George Eliot

Don't let someone else's opinion of you become your reality. - Les Brown

. . .

If you're not positive energy, you're negative energy. - Mark Cuban

I am not a product of my circumstances. I am a product of my decisions. - Stephen R. Covey

The greatest discovery of my generation is that a human being can alter his life by altering his attitudes. - William James

One of the differences between some successful and unsuccessful people is that one group is full of doers, while the other is full of wishers. - Edmond Mbiaka

I'd rather regret the things I've done than regret the things I haven't done. - Lucille Ball

You cannot plow a field by turning it over in your mind. To begin, begin. - Gordon B. Hinckley

When you arise in the morning think of what a privilege it is to be alive, to think, to enjoy, to love. - Marcus Aurelius

Mondays are the start of the work week which offer new beginnings 52 times a year. - David Dweck

Be miserable. Or motivate yourself. Whatever must be done, it's always your choice. - Wayne Dyer

. . .

You can get everything in life you want if you will just help enough other people get what they want. - Zig Ziglar

Inspiration does exist, but it must find you working. - Pablo Picasso

Don't settle for average. Bring your best to the moment. Then, whether it fails or succeeds, at least you know you gave all you had. - Angela Bassett

Show up, show up, show up, and after a while the muse shows up, too. - Isabel Allende

Yes, I am a nice person, but if you cross the line too many times everything can change very quickly. – Keanu Reeves

You cannot fix someone who doesn't want to be fixed, but you can ruin your life trying. - Anonymous

You can't go back and change the beginning. But you can start where you are and change the ending. – C. S. Lewis

You can easily judge the character if a man by how he treats those who can do nothing for him. – Johann wolf gang Vo Goethe

Don't bunt. Aim out of the ballpark. Aim for the company of immortals. - David Ogilvy

. . .

If you believe something needs to exist, if it's something you want to use yourself, don't let anyone ever stop you from doing it. - Tobias Lütke

Don't look at your feet to see if you are doing it right. Just dance. - Anne Lamott

Someone's sitting in the shade today because someone planted a tree a long time ago. - Warren Buffet

True freedom is impossible without a mind made free by discipline. - Mortimer J. Adler

Rivers know this: there is no hurry. We shall get there some day. - A.A. Milne

There is a vitality, a life force, an energy, a quickening that is translated through you into action, and because there is only one of you in all time, this expression is unique. And if you block it, it will never exist through any other medium and will be lost. - Martha Graham

Small is not just a stepping-stone. Small is a great destination itself. - Jason Fried

. . .

He that can have patience can have what he will. - Benjamin Franklin

The only one who can tell you "You can't win" is you and you don't have to listen. - Jessica Ennis

Set your goals high, and don't stop till you get there. - Bo Jackson

Take your victories, whatever they may be, cherish them, use them, but don't settle for them. - Mia Hamm

It's fine to celebrate success but it is more important to heed the lessons of failure. - Bill Gates

I can't tell you how many times I've been given a no. Only to find that a better, brighter, bigger yes was right around the corner. - Arlan Hamilton

We need to accept that we won't always make the right decisions, that we'll screw up royally sometimes understanding that failure is not the opposite of success, it's part of success. - Ariana Huffington

When everything seems to be going against you, remember that the airplane takes off against the wind, not with it. - Henry Ford

You cannot always control what goes on outside. But you can always control what goes on inside. - Wayne Dyer

. . .

We are what we repeatedly do. Excellence, then, is not an act, but a habit. - Aristotle

Start where you are. Use what you have. Do what you can. - Arthur Ashe

Hustle beats talent when talent doesn't hustle. - Ross Simmonds

Everything you've ever wanted is sitting on the other side of fear. - George Addair

The question isn't who is going to let me; it's who is going to stop me. - Ayn Rand

Every strike brings me closer to the next home run. - Babe Ruth

I have not failed. I've just found 10,000 ways that won't work. - Thomas A. Edison

Don't worry about failure; you only have to be right once. - Drew Houston

You carry the passport to your own happiness. - Diane von Furstenberg

. . .

Never let success get to your head and never let failure get to your heart. - Drake

Ideation without execution is delusion. - Robin Sharma

Make sure your worst enemy doesn't live between your own two ears. - Laird Hamilton

It is a rough road that leads to the heights of greatness. - Lucius Annaeus Seneca

For the great doesn't happen through impulse alone and is a succession of little things that are brought together. - Vincent van Gogh

If we take care of the moments, the years will take care of themselves. - Maria Edgeworth

Sometimes magic is just someone spending more time on something than anyone else might reasonably expect. - Raymond Joseph Teller

It's not the will to win those matters, everyone has that. It's the will to prepare to win those matters. - Paul Bryant

As a single footstep will not make a path on the earth, so a single thought will not make a pathway in the mind. To make a deep physical path, we walk repeatedly. To make a deep mental path, we must think over and over the kind of thoughts we wish to dominate our lives. - Henry David Thoreau

Never give up on a dream just because of the time it will take to accomplish it. The time will pass anyway. - Earl Nightingale

True humility is not thinking less of yourself; it is thinking of yourself less. - C.S. Lewis

The two most important days in your life are the day you're born and the day you find out why. - Mark Twain

Nothing ever goes away until it teaches us what we need to know. - Pema Chodron

We can see through others only when we can see through ourselves. – Bruce Lee

First forget inspiration. Habit is more dependable. Habit will sustain you whether you're inspired or not. Habit will help you finish and polish your stories. Inspiration won't. Habit is persistence in practice. - Octavia Butler

The best way out is always through. - Robert Frost

. . .

The battles that count aren't the ones for gold medals. The struggles within yourself, the invisible, inevitable battles inside all of us, that's where it's at. - Jesse Owens

If there is no struggle, there is no progress. - Frederick Douglass

Someone will declare, "I am the leader!" and expect everyone to get in line and follow him or her to the gates of heaven or hell. My experience is that it doesn't happen that way. Others follow you based on the quality of your actions rather than the magnitude of your declarations. - Bill Walsh

Courage is like a muscle. We strengthen it by use. - Ruth Gordo

Relentlessly prune bullshit, don't wait to do things that matter, and savor the time you have. That's what you do when life is short. - Paul Graham

More is lost by indecision than wrong decision. - Marcus Tullius Cicero

If the highest aim of a captain were to preserve his ship, he would keep it in port forever. - Thomas Aquinas

You can be the ripest, juiciest peach in the world, and there's still going to be somebody who hates peaches. - Dita Von Teese

. . .

Keep a little fire burning; however small, however hidden. - Cormac McCarthy

You'll never get bored when you try something new. There's really no limit to what you can do. - Dr. Seuss

I think it's intoxicating when somebody is so unapologetically who they are. - Don Cheadle

You can never leave footprints that last if you are always walking on tiptoe. - Leymah Mbowe

If you don't like the road you're walking, start paving another one. - Dolly Parton

If it makes you nervous, you're doing it right. - Childish Gambino

What you do makes a difference, and you have to decide what kind of difference you want to make. - Jane Goodall

I choose to make the rest of my life the best of my life. - Louise Hay

In order to be irreplaceable, one must always be different. - Coco Chanel

. . .

Anything can make me stop and look and wonder, and sometimes learn. - Kurt Vonnegut

People's passion and desire for authenticity is strong. - Constance Wu

A surplus of effort could overcome a deficit of confidence. - Sonia Sotomayor

Doubt is a killer. You just have to know who you are and what you stand for. - Jennifer Lopez

No one changes the world who isn't obsessed. - Billie Jean King

I learned a long time ago that there is something worse than missing the goal, and that's not pulling the trigger. - Mia Hamm

Some people want it to happen, some wish it would happen, others make it happen. - Michael Jordan

The two most important days in your life are the day you're born and the day you find out why. - Mark Twain

Nothing ever goes away until it teaches us what we need to know. - Pema Chodron

. . .

We can see through others only when we can see through ourselves.
- Bruce Lee

First forget inspiration. Habit is more dependable. Habit will sustain you whether you're inspired or not. Habit will help you finish and polish your stories. Inspiration won't. Habit is persistence in practice. - Octavia Butler

The best way out is always through. - Robert Frost

The battles that count aren't the ones for gold medals. The struggles within yourself, the invisible, inevitable battles inside all of us that's where it's at. - Jesse Owens

If there is no struggle, there is no progress. - Frederick Douglass

Someone will declare, "I am the leader!" and expect everyone to get in line and follow him or her to the gates of heaven or hell. My experience is that it doesn't happen that way. Others follow you based on the quality of your actions rather than the magnitude of your declarations. - Bill Walsh

Courage is like a muscle. We strengthen it by use. - Ruth Gordo

Relentlessly prune bullshit, don't wait to do things that matter, and savor the time you have. That's what you do when life is short. - Paul Graham

. . .

When you're born in a burning house, you think the whole world is on fire. But it'd not. – Richard Kadrey

Forever. I love that forever doesn't exist. But we have a word for it anyways, and use it all the time. It's beautiful and doomed, - Viv Albertine

More is lost by indecision than wrong decision. - Marcus Tullius Cicero

If the highest aim of a captain were to preserve his ship, he would keep it in port forever. - Thomas Aquinas

You can be the ripest, juiciest peach in the world, and there's still going to be somebody who hates peaches. - Dita Von Teese

Keep a little fire burning; however small, however hidden. - Cormac McCarthy

You'll never get bored when you try something new. There's really no limit to what you can do. - Dr. Seuss

I think it's intoxicating when somebody is so unapologetically who they are. - Don Cheadle

You can never leave footprints that last if you are always walking on tiptoe. - Leymah Mbowe

. . .

If you don't like the road you're walking, start paving another one. - Dolly Parton

If it makes you nervous, you're doing it right. - Childish Gambino

What you do makes a difference, and you have to decide what kind of difference you want to make. - Jane Goodall

I choose to make the rest of my life the best of my life. - Louise Hay

In order to be irreplaceable, one must always be different. - Coco Chanel

Anything can make me stop and look and wonder, and sometimes learn. - Kurt Vonnegut

People's passion and desire for authenticity is strong. - Constance Wu

A surplus of effort could overcome a deficit of confidence. - Sonia Sotomayor

Doubt is a killer. You just have to know who you are and what you stand for. - Jennifer Lopez

. . .

No one changes the world who isn't obsessed. - Billie Jean King

I learned a long time ago that there is something worse than missing the goal, and that's not pulling the trigger. - Mia Hamm

Some people want it to happen, some wish it would happen, others make it happen. - Michael Jordan

Half of life is lost in charming others. The other half is lost in going through anxieties caused by others. Leave this play, you have played enough. - Rumi

Don't speak negatively about yourself, even as a joke. Your body doesn't know the difference. Words are energy and cast spells, that's why it's called spelling. Change the way you speak about yourself and you can change your life. What you're not changing, you're also choosing. - Bruce Lee

People who don't have goals work for people who do. - Jack Canfield

One of the best lessons you can learn in life is to master how to remain calm. Calm is a superpower. - Bruce Lee

There are only two people who can tell you the truth about yourself; an enemy who has

. . .

All the problems are stuck between "Mind" and "Matter." If you don't "Mind", it doesn't "Matter." - Dr. Hunter

Don't cry over the past. Don't stress about the future. Live in the present and make it beautiful for yourself and others. - Pema Woser

If you give your trust to a person who does not deserve it, you actually give him the power to destroy you. – Khaled Saad

A person who never made a mistake, never tried anything new. – Albert Einstein

No matter how many mistakes you make or how slow you progress, you are still way of everyone who isn't trying. – Tony Robbins

It is our attitude at the beginning of a difficult task which more than anything else will affect its successful outcome. – William James

If money is your hope for independence, you will never have it. The only real security that a man will have in this world is a reserve of knowledge, experience, and ability. - Henry Ford

The bad news is time flies. He good news is you're the pilot. – Michael Altshuler

Be courageous. Challenge orthodoxy. Stand up for what you believe in. When you are in your rocking chair talking tm your grandchildren many years from now, be sure you have a good story to tell. – Amal Clooney

Success is not final; failure is not fatal. It is te courage to continue that counts. – Winson Churchill

Resilience is when you address uncertainty with flexibility. - Anonymous

Your mind will always believe everything that you tell it. Feed it truth. Feed it hope. Feed it with love. – Anonymous

Work until your bank account looks like a phone number. - Anonymous

The strongest actions for a woman are to love herself, be herself and shine amongst those who never believed she could. – Anonymous

You learn more from failure than from success. Don't let it stop you. Failure builds character. - Anonymous

He who blames others has a long way to go on his journey. He who blames himself is halfway there. He who blames no one has arrived. - Chinese Proverb

A crisis is an opportunity riding the dangerous wind. - Chinese Proverb

. . .

It's better to be without a book than to believe a book entirely. - Chinese Proverb

A little impatience will spoil great plans. - Chinese Proverb

If you bow at all, bow low. - Chinese Proverb

A journey of a thousand miles begins with a single step. - Chinese Proverb

A smile will gain you ten more years of life. - Chinese Proverb

A bird not sing because it has an answer. It sings because it has a song. - Chinese Proverb

Talk does not cook rice. - Chinese Proverb

A man who cannot tolerate small misfortunes can never accomplish great things. - Chinese Proverb

Experience is a comb which nature give us when awe is bold. - Chinese Proverb

. . .

Be not afraid of growing slowly, be afraid only of standing still. - Chinese Proverb

He who asks is a fool for five minutes, but he who does not ask remains fool forever. - Chinese Proverb

It is a myth that you need to rise and shine to have a good start to a day. You can roll around in bed thinking about friends like me and you will still have a great start to the day. – Anonymous

Life is short, fragile and does not wait for anyone. There will NEVER be a perfect time to pursue your dreams and goals. – Anonymous

If the plan doesn't work, change the plan, but never the goal. – Anonymous

Be happy not because everything is perfect. But because you choose to focus on the perfect moments. – Anonymous

Stay positive. Better days are on their way. – Anonymous

"LISTEN" and "SILENT" are spelled with the same letters. Think about it. – Anonymous

They laugh at me because I'm different. I laugh at them because they are all the same. – Anonymous

. . .

Success is a vehicle, which moves on a wheel named hard work, but the journey is impossible without the fuel named self-confidence. – Anonymous

Even when you fully trust someone. Don't tell them everything. – Anonymous

Accept both compliments and criticism. It takes both sun and rain for a flower to grow. – Anonymous

Don't allow someone to treat you poorly just because you love them. – Anonymous

Happiness is the new rich. Inner peace is the new success. Health is the new wealth. Kindness is the new cool. – Anonymous

As long you are breathing, everything is possible. Never quit trying. Make the rest of your life, the best of your life. – Anonymous

Every little smile can touch someone's heart. No one is born happy, but all of us are born with ability to Always Be Happy. – Anonymous

You will meet two kinds of people in life: ones who build you up and ones who tear you down. But in the end, you'll thank them both. - Anonymous

. . .

Leadership is not about being the best. Leadership is about making everyone else better. – Anonymous

Don't let anyone who hasn't been in your shoes tell you how to tie your laces. – Anonymous

Never re-friend a person that has tried to destroy your character, your money, or your relationships. A snake only sheds its skin to become a bigger snake. - Anonymous

A satisfied life is better than a successful life because our success is measured by others, but our satisfaction is measured by our own soul, mind and heart. - Anonymous

If you aim for nothing, you'll hit it every time. – Anonymous

Remember why you started. – Anonymous

You have to believe it before you see it. – Anonymous If you don't have big dreams and goals, you'll end up working for someone that does. – Anonymous

Eyes are useless when the mind is blind. – Anonymous

. . .

Moving on doesn't mean you forget about things. It just means you have to accept what happened and continue living. - Anonymous

We learn something from everyone who passes through our lives. Some lessons are painful, some painless, but all are priceless. – Anonymous

Some people in your family will come miles to bury you, but won't even cross a street to support you when you are alive. – Anonymous

Take care of yourself. Go for a walk, get a haircut, eat your favorite food, read a book, cry if you need to and take a vacation. Do what you need to do. Take care of yourself, because at the end of the day, you all you've get. Keep going forward. - Anonymous

Before you start to judge me, step into my shoes and walk the life I'm living and if you get as far as I am, just maybe you will see how strong I really am. – Anonymous

Never beg to a friendship or a relationship with anyone. If you don't receive the same effort you give. Cut them off. – Anonymous

If you can't fly, run. If you can't run, walk. If you can't walk, craw! But by all means, keep moving. – Anonymous

More often in life, we end up regretting the chances in life that we had, but didn't take them, than those chances that we took and wished we hadn't. – Anonymous

. . .

A truly rich man is one whose children run into his arms when his hands are empty. – Anonymous

You learn more from failure than from success. Don't let it stop you. Failure builds character. – Anonymous

Everyone makes mistakes in life, but that doesn't mean they have to pay for them the rest of their life. Sometimes good people make bad choices. It doesn't mean they are bad. It means they are human. – Anonymous

The hardest walk is walking alone, but it's also the walk that makes you the strongest. – Anonymous

The most important lesson I've learned so far is: "Don't let anyone make you cruel. No matter how badly you want to give the world a taste of their bitter medicine. It is never worth losing yourself. – Anonymous

Having one hundred friends is too few. Having even one foe is too much. – Anonymous

When you destroy someone's life with lies take it as a loan. It will come back to you with interest. – Anonymous

. . .

Your perception of me is a reflex ion of you. And my reaction to you is an awareness of you. – Anonymous

One of the biggest lies ever told is, "Blood makes you family." No, blood makes you related. Loyalty, love send trust make you family. – Anonymous

People are jealous of you because your character carries more weight than their titles. – Anonymous

I admire people who choose to shine even after all the storms they have been through. – Anonymous

Sing like no one's listening, love like you've never been hurt, dance like nobody's watching, and live like its heaven on earth. - Anonymous

Your best teacher is your last mistake. – Anonymous

Everyone makes mistakes in life, but that doesn't mean they have to pay for them for the rest of their life. Sometimes, good people make bad choices. It doesn't mean they're human. – Anonymous

Accept your past without regret, handle your present with confidence, and face your future without fear. – Anonymous

. . .

One of the hardest lessons in life is letting go. Whether it's guilt, anger, love, loss or betrayal. Change is never easy. We fight to hold on and we fight to let go. – Anonymous

I have fought a thousand battles, but I'm still standing. I have cried a thousand tears but I'm still smiling. I have betrayed and rejected, but I still walk proud. I smile, I laugh, I love hard. I am humble. I am beautiful. I am real. I am me. – Anonymous

Never give up on a dream just because of the time it will take to accomplish it. - Anonymous

There is a point in your life when you realize who matters, who never did, who won't anymore, and who always will. And in the end, you earn who is fake, who is true and who would risk it all for you. – Anonymous

It's never too late for a new beginning in your life. – Anonymous

If you don't leave your past in the past, it will destroy your future. Live for what today has to offer, not for what yesterday has taken away. – Anonymous

Don't walk behind me. I may not lead. Don't walk in front of me. I may not follow. Just walk beside me and be my friend. – Anonymous

. . .

You cannot control everything that happens to you; you can only control the way you respond to what happens. In your response is your power. - Anonymous

You will meet two kinds of people in life: ones who build you up and ones who tear you down. But in the end, you'll thank them both. - Anonymous

It is impossible to live without failing at something, unless you live so cautiously, that you might as well not have lived at all – in which case you fail by default. - Anonymous

The one who falls and gets up is do much stronger than the one who never fell. - Anonymous

Be thankful for the little things. – Anonymous

If you stay positive in a negative situation, you win. – Anonymous

Holding onto anger is like drinking poison and expecting the other person die. – Anonymous

The trials you encounter will introduce you to your strengths. Remain steadfast and one day you will build something that endures. Something worthy of your potential. – Anonymous

. . .

A special friend is hand to find, hard to lose and impossible to forget. True friends are never apart. May be in distance, but not in the heart. – Anonymous

Life is too short. We don't know when will die. It doesn't matter how long we live. What matters most is how we lived our life. Be kind, be generous. Be humble because it adds value to your life. – Anonymous

There will be hard days. But they won't last forever. – Anonymous

Everybody isn't your friend. Just because they hand around you and laugh with you doesn't mean they are your friends. At the end of the day, real situations expose fake people, so pay attention. – Anonymous

When a toxic person can no longer control you, they will try to control how others see you. The misinformation will feel unfair, but stay above it trusting that other people will eventually see the truth, just like you did. – Anonymous

One day or day one, you decide. – Anonymous

Everyone must choose one of the two pains: The pain of discipline or the pain of regret. – Anonymous

Eyes are useless when the mind is blind. – Anonymous

. . .

If they make an option, make them your history. – Anonymous

People will notice the change in your attitude towards them, but won't notice their behavior that make your change. – Anonymous

A special friend is hand to find, hard to lose and impossible to forget. True friends are never apart. May be in distance, but not in the heart. – Anonymous

Life is too short. We don't know when will die. It doesn't matter how long we live. What matters most is how we lived our life. Be kind, be generous. Be humble because it adds value to your life. – Anonymous

There will be hard days. But they won't last forever. – Anonymous

Everybody isn't your friend. Just because they hand around you and laugh with you doesn't mean they are your friends. At the end of the day, real situations expose fake people, so pay attention. – Anonymous

Whenever you do, don't get stuck on the thing that ruins your day. Smile and be grateful. Life is too short to waste on negativity. – Anonymous

You can't force someone to respect you, but you can refuse to get disrespected. – Anonymous

. . .

There is a point in your life when you realize who matters, who never did, who won't anymore, and who always will. And in the end, you earn who is fake, who is true and who would risk it all for you. – Anonymous

It's never too late for a new beginning in your life. – Anonymous

Never tell your problem to anyone. 20% don't care and the other 80% are glad you have those problems. – Anonymous

If you fail, never give up because F.A.I.L. means, "First Attempt in Learning." E.N.D. means, "Effort Never Dies." If you get NO as an answer, remember, N.O. means "Next Opportunity." So, let's be Positive. – Anonymous

Remember, most of your stress comes from the way life is. Adjust your attitude, and all that extra stress is gone. – Anonymous

In absence of clearly defined goals, we become strangely loyal to performing daily acts of trivia. – Anonymous

It is fruitless to wish you started years ago. In the future you will wish you had started today. – Anonymous

A satisfied life is better than a successful life. Because our success is measured by others, but your satisfaction is measured by our own soul, mind and heart. – Anonymous

. . .

Never explain yourself to anyone. Because the person who likes you doesn't need it, and the person who dislikes you won't believe it. – Anonymous

Don't cry over the past, it's gone. Don't stress about the future, it hasn't arrived. Live in the present and make it beautiful. – Anonymous

If you don't learn leave your past in the past, it will destroy your future. Live for what today has to offer, not what yesterday has taken away. – Anonymous

Life is the most difficult exam. Many people fail because they try to copy others, not realizing that everyone has a different question paper. – Anonymous

If you don't leave your past in the past, it will destroy your future. Live for what today has to offer, not for what yesterday has taken away. – Anonymous

Hate has 4 letters, so does Love. Enemies has 7 letters, so does Friends. Lying has 5 letters, so does the Truth. Negative has 8 letters, so does Positive. Under has 5 letters, so does Above. Cry has 3 letters, so does Joy. Anger has 5 letters, so does Happy. Right has 5 letters, so does Wrong. Hurt has 4 letters, so does Heal. This means life is like double edged sword. So, transform every negative side into an aura of positivity. We choose the better side of the life. – Anonymous

. . .

A relationship means that you come together to make each other better. Believe in each other. Build each other. Be their peace, not their problem. – Anonymous

Forget who hurt you, who betrayed you, don't let break you. But don't forget what it taught you, don't even put yourself in that position again. – Anonymous

Bridge and wall are made with the same material. But bridge joins the people and wall divides the people. Choose the Right one. – Anonymous

In the blink of an eye everything can change. So, forgive often and love with all your heart, take no one for granted for you never know what may happen tomorrow. – Anonymous

Spend your time on those that love you unconditionally. Don't waste it on those that only love you when conditions are right for them. – Anonymous

The biggest lesson you can learn is that nobody is going to remember what you wore or what your jewelry was like. But what they are going to remember is how you treated them. And that's the biggest lesson in life. How you treat people. That is the legacy you leave behind. – Anonymous

Don't compare your life to others. There is no comparison between the sun and moon. They shine what it's their time. – Anonymous

. . .

Your mind is a magnet. If you always think of blessings, you attract more blessings. If you always think of problems, you attract more problems. Always keep good thoughts and always be positive. – Anonymous

Your journey is not the same as mine, and my journey is not yours. But if you meet me on a certain path, may we encourage each other. – Anonymous

You never realize how strong you are. Until being strong is the only choice you have. – Anonymous

Before you go to sleep tonight, remember an entire sea of water can't sink a ship, unless it gets inside the ship. Similarly, the negativity of the world can't put you down unless you allow it to get inside your head. – Anonymous

Anyone can give up. It's the easiest thing in the world to do. But to hold it together when everyone else would understand and if you feel apart that's the true strength. – Anonymous

Fear: You see an opportunity that is literally calling your name, but you ignore it because you need more information. Instead of ceasing the opportunity you hesitate, delay, procrastinate, bury your head in the sand, and by the time you lift up your head, the opportunity is gone. The rich take action with 40%-60% information and their gut feeling. It's called taking a risk. To be successful and rich, start taking risks and taking advantage of opportunities around you. - Anonymous

. . .

Hate has 4 letters, so does Love. Enemies has 7 letters, so does Friends. Lying has You can't fall if you don't climb. But there's no joy in living your whole life on the ground. - Anonymous

The point is that you don't know how much future you got. What's gone is gone. There's absolutely nothing you can do about it. Some of you have had divorces. – Anonymous

I hope you win the wars you tell no one about. – Anonymous

A person who left in anger will always comeback. But one the who left with a smile will never comeback. - Anonymous

It is impossible to live without failing at something, unless you live so cautiously, that you might as well not have lived at all in which case you fail by default. - Anonymous

You cannot control everything that happens to you; you can only control the way you respond to what happens. In your response is your power. - Anonymous

Life is not about who you once were. It's about who you are now, and who you have the potential to be. - Anonymous

Never take life seriously. Nobody gets out alive anyway. – Anonymous

. . .

The most expensive liquid in the world is a tear. It's 1% water and 99% feelings. Think before you hurt someone. - Anonymous

Stay positive. Better days are on their way. - Anonymous

5 letters, so does the Truth. Negative has 8 letters. So does Positive. Under has 5 letters, so does Above. Cry has 3 letters, so does Joy. Anger has 5 letters, so does Happy. Right has 5 letters, so does Wrong. Hurt has 4 letters, so does Heal. This means life is like double edged sword. So, transform every negative side into an aura of positivity. We choose the better side of the life. - Anonymous

There is a point in your life when you realize who matters, who never did, who won't anymore, and who always will. And in the end, you earn who is fake, who is true and who would risk it all for you. - Anonymous

Never expect to get what you give what you give, not everyone has a heart like you. - Anonymous

A positive mind finds opportunity in everything. A negative mind finds fault in everything. – Anonymous

Every little smile can touch someone's heart. No one is born happy, but all of us are born with ability to Always Be Happy. – Anonymous

Do good and good will come to you. – Anonymous

. . .

Until the rotten tooth is pulled out, one must learn to chew with caution. - African Proverbs

No matter how long a log stays in the water, it does not become a crocodile. The meaning, you will be always be who you are, regardless of how long your fake character. - African proverb

If you wish to move mountains tomorrow, you must start by lifting stones today. - African Proverb

A wise man never knows all, only fools know everything. - African Proverb

When a bird builds a nest, it uses the feathers of other birds. Meaning: We have to cooperate with other people to get everything done in life. - African Proverb

The best answer will come from the person who is not angry. – Arabic Proverb

The best time to plant a tree was 20 years ago. The second-best time is now. – Chinese Proverb

The person who says it cannot be done should not interrupt the person who is doing it. – Chinese Proverb

. . .

The best advice is found is found on the pillow. – Danish Proverb

Coffee and love taste best when hot. – Ethiopian Proverb

Begin to weave and God will give you the thread. – German Proverb

Whoever gets burned by soup, blows on yogurt. – Greek Proverb

The donkey called the rooster big-headed. – Greek Proverb

Unripe grape gets sweet as honey, at a slow pace. – Greek Proverb

When the cat's away, the mice dance. – Greek Proverb

People who do not see each other frequently, they soon forget each other. – Greek Proverb

The camel can't see her own hump. – Greek Proverb

From outside the dance-circle, you sing a lot of songs. – Greek Proverb

The tongue/language has no bones, but bones it crushes. – Greek Proverb

. . .

Too many opinions sink the boat. – Greek Proverb

My home, my little home, a little house of my own. – Greek Proverb

Many words are poverty. – Greek Proverb

Fall seven times and stand up eight. – Japanese Proverb

Don't speak bad of yourself. For the warrior within hears your words and is lessened by them. - Japanese Samurai Proverb

If the wind will not serve, take to the oars. – Latin Proverb

The rubbish we speak is like froth on the water, actions are drops of gold. - Tibetan Proverb

The rubbish we speak is like froth on the water, actions are drops of gold. -Tibetan Proverb

Time is the best doctor. – Yiddish proverb

Sing like no one's listening, love like you've never been hurt, dance like nobody's watching, and live like its heaven on earth. – (Attributed to various sources)